7
DEADLY
SINS

7 DEADLY SINS

A VERY PARTIAL LIST

Aviad Kleinberg

Translated by Susan Emanuel in collaboration

with the author

The Belknap Press of

HARVARD UNIVERSITY PRESS

Cambridge, Massachusetts, and London, England

2008

A Caravan book. For more information, visit *www.caravanbooks.org.*

This book was originally published as *Péchés Capitaux,*
copyright © 2008 by Editions du Seuil, Paris.

Library of Congress Cataloging-in-Publication Data
Kleinberg, Aviad M.
    [Péchés capitaux. English]
    Seven deadly sins : a very partial list / Aviad Kleinberg : translated
by Susan Emanuel in collaboration with the author.
        p. cm.
    Includes bibliographical references and index.
    ISBN-13: 978-0-674-03141-8 (hardcover : alk. paper)
    1. Deadly sins.   2. Sin.   3. Sins.   I. Title.
    BV4626.K5313   2008
    241'.3—dc22   2008016574

Contents

7
DEADLY
SINS

THE LIZARD'S TAIL

There is no sin without context. There is no sin in itself. The very notion of sin is always the result of a comparison, explicit or implicit, between a specific ideal and a specific reality. Without this comparison, in which an act is weighed in the moral balance and found wanting, there is no sin—there are only actions and passions. Human actions and passions become sins only in a given moral and cultural context. As contexts and rules shift, so does the definition of sin. What once constituted a sin (masturbation, for example) ceases to be wrong; what once did *not* constitute a sin (beating up young children or selling human beings) ceases to be right. Right and wrong are continually defined and redefined by society. The moral balance tilts toward one direction, then toward the other. Morality expresses itself in absolute terms: "Never" and "Always." It presents itself as a seamless, timeless garment. A closer look reveals the seams of time and place. Sin is a cultural construct.

Strata of ideas, beliefs, and preconceived notions are features of every culture. We observe the world, and ourselves, from the uppermost stratum: the present. But the lower strata, saturated with the past, have not disappeared. The present is nothing but the latest aggregation from past events and processes. Our roots traverse all the layers of our sedimented culture. In pushing up toward the present, contemporary notions are imbued with the stains of our fathers—with someone else's recollections, someone else's guilt. Worse still, we are not a chorus singing in cultural unison; we are would-be soloists stubbornly singing off-key. Ethical imperatives are addressed to collectives, but ethical choices are always individual. In the realm of right and wrong, everything is personal.

Every person is an accident, a collision between individual impulses and cultural options. Before attaining the age of reason, we absorb, without real examination or scrutiny, the internal contradictions of our environment. The irresponsible judgments, the arbitrary assessments, the passing remarks of adults are filtered through our immature minds, then mixed with a powerful blend of emotional likes and dislikes, and little by little our moral fiber makes its hesitant appearance. Reaching maturity, we try to impose order on the affective and moral chaos of our childhood, the impossible compromises and contradictory urges, the personal aches and general anxieties. We try to be reasonable.

It is not easy to be reasonable. The ground seems to slip away beneath our feet. The custodians of public morality try to mandate their own balance, to decree absolute values where everything is relative, to proclaim clarity where everything is obscure, to declare objectivity where everything is subjective. They brandish their moral timetables, promising that those who arrive on time at the station will safely reach their moral destination. We always arrive too early or too late. We are too quick to forgive ourselves the unforgivable, and too willing to let the sour grapes of our fathers set our teeth on edge.[1] We sin in our own individual fashion, breaking rules made especially for us. Succeeding or failing, we do it our way.

There is no sin without context. And there is no impersonal writing on sin. All writing on sin is autobiographical, even when the writer analyzes abstract ideas or discusses the sins of others. This book is not a confession. To a certain extent, it is a way to avoid confession. Yet the book does deal with me, especially when I am not speaking about myself.

When does the awareness of sin arise in us? When does infantile narcissism—the conviction that everything belongs to us, that any pleasure and satisfaction denied us constitutes a moral scandal—transform itself into a feeling of guilt, into a sensation that we have done evil in the eyes of the Lord and of men? Freud thought that this awareness emerges together with the Ego, with the realization that the child is not the flesh of its mother, that the separation between mother and child is definitive and irreparable. Feelings of insufficiency constitute a basic element of human personality. We understand that we are not all-powerful. We recognize the primary mortal failings—weakness, solitude, and despair—for it is those (not pride, envy, and anger) that constitute the prototypes of sin. We measure ourselves against our impossible dreams of perfection, and the paradise of wishful thinking (to be always whole, to be always without fear or pain, to be always satisfied) and we find ourselves wanting. We suffer. We realize that we have been punished. All suffering is punishment. We search for the reasons for this punishment. "God of Mercy, we have sinned before You. Have pity on us."

But is it right to begin like that, with universal reflections—not with this particular man, Aviad Kleinberg, but with Everyman? Is it honest to start with generalities, beyond the embarrassing particulars of memory, beyond the body, beyond the body of evidence? Surely this is wrong. There is no sin without context, no writing on sin that is not autobiographical.

In primary school I had a classmate called Micky. He was lonelier than me and much weaker. I was endowed with considerable physical strength and with a talent for sarcasm. This did not win me many friends, but it was usually enough to paralyze my adversaries. While we were all trying to become (each according to his possibilities and inclinations) caricatures of the typical Israeli macho, Micky remained a withdrawn infant, living somewhat autistically in his own world. He neither tried to be like the others, nor blatantly challenged conventions, as I did from time to time when I was fed up with my own efforts to make myself accepted. Micky was quite simply himself. He sketched odd, delicate drawings in his notebooks and built miniature cities in the sand. His cities were a tangle of roads among twigs and bits of wood, minuscule electrical poles made from popsicle sticks, vaguely defined buildings of matchboxes, and tiny bridges over Lilliputian rivers of sand. Without complaint, he bore the endless ridicule and contempt heaped upon him from all sides. He would laugh his strange laugh and go his own way.

Micky built his towns in all sorts of places. The ones he constructed in the schoolyard were systematically destroyed by the other children. To give free reign to his urban creativity, Micky built another town in a wadi (a small ravine) near his neighborhood, far from the barbarians' eyes. In those days I often roamed the wastelands that extended between the neighborhoods of my hometown, Beer Sheva. In school you had to be either "north" or "south." I was neither. My family lived between neighborhoods, and I felt at home only in geographic and social No-Man's-Land. For hours I would walk by myself, desperately trying to make sense of my loneliness, dreaming of vindication. Every day I hoped that something would happen and I would be saved, that I would stumble upon something good, that the pain would stop, that the circle of solitude would break. Micky's miniature city was located far from the usual circuits of the *hevre*, the guys. But it was on my path. It was much bigger than his other urban creations, and one could see that he had put a great deal of time and effort into it.

I remember studying that magnificent construction for a while, and then destroying it. I knocked down everything—roads, bridges, trees. I don't think I enjoyed the destruction. I'm quite sure I was immediately invaded by a strong feeling of shame. I understood that I had become just like the barbarians, the classmates I both detested and envied. For Immanuel Kant, awareness of the wickedness of one's act transforms it into "radical evil"—a wrong stemming neither from oversight nor from thoughtlessness, but committed with full understanding of the moral fault it embodies.[2]

I cannot pretend to have surrendered to social pressure. That act of destruction was not a means for gaining acceptance by a gang. Later in life, I was occasionally pressured to harm other people—women, Arabs, weak individuals—in order to prove my toughness, my manhood, my solidarity to the group. I always refused to do so. But in school, I did not belong to any group. Indeed, not-belonging was my main attribute. Besides, nobody knew I had destroyed the little city—not even Micky—and I find it hard to believe that my feat of senseless vandalism would have impressed boys. I was not performing a social rite of passage. This was solitary trespassing. Years later, I came upon the famous passage in Saint Augustine's *Confessions* where he recounts an episode of stealing pears in his native town of Thagaste (in present-day Algeria). Some years ago I even translated the *Confessions* from Latin into Hebrew.[3] Here is the description from Book 2:

> There was a pear tree near our vineyard laden with fruit, though attractive in neither color nor taste. To shake the fruit off the tree and carry off the pears, I and a gang of naughty adolescents set off late at night after (in our pestilential way) we had continued our game in the streets. We carried off a huge load of pears. But they were not for our feasts but merely to throw to the pigs. Even if we ate a few, nevertheless our pleasure lay in doing what was not allowed. Such was my heart, O God, such was my heart. You had pity on it when it was at the bottom of the abyss. Now let my heart tell you what it was seeking there in that I became evil for no reason. I had no motive for my wickedness except wickedness itself. It was foul, and I loved it. I

loved the self-destruction, I loved my fall, not the object
for which I had fallen but my fall itself. My depraved soul
leaped down from your firmament to ruin. It was seeking
not to gain anything by shameful means, but shame for its
own sake.[4]

Setting aside, for the moment, the psychological and ethical questions raised by Augustine's description, I would like to focus on the basic assumption underlying this text. Augustine is certain that the rules
of the ethical game are clear and that a man who is honest with himself always knows the specific weight of each of his acts. For him, there
is no Freudian denial; there are only lies. What is more, evil is never
banal; it is *always* radical.[5] Misdemeanors, like stealing worthless pears,
may be insignificant so far as their consequences are concerned, but
the motivation that underlies them is not really different from that
which pushes us to horrible crimes. We love evil for its own sake. And
our faults are never really hidden. God walks in our gardens and His
spirit hovers over our abysses. He sees, remembers, and exacts accounts. The intrusive presence of God in the Augustinian world para-
doxically transforms intentional evil into a heroic act, tragic in that it is
essentially without hope. It is impossible to contest the tyranny of divine justice, impossible to escape punishment. The sinner brings about
his own ruin in the name of an impossible and absurd desire for freedom.[6]

"Therefore in that act of theft what was the object of my love, and
in what way did I viciously and perversely imitate my Lord?" wonders
Saint Augustine.

Was my pleasure to break your law by deceit since I had not
the power to do that by force? Was I acting like a prisoner
with restricted liberty who does without punishment what
is not permitted, thereby making an assertion of possessing a dim resemblance to omnipotence? Here is a runaway

slave fleeing his master and pursuing a shadow [Job 7:2].
What rottenness! What a monstrous life and what an abyss
of death! Was it possible to take pleasure in what was illicit
for no reason other than that it was not allowed?[7]

Sin can be the expression of an ardent desire for freedom, for liberation
from any rules but the rules of our own desire. In its most heroic manifestations it becomes an act of creation—creation of the individual self
at the price of being cast out of the common paradise. Milton's Satan is
a tragic hero who can create only by the sole means that the Almighty
leaves him: destruction, and especially self-destruction. But in order
for one to be the Devil, there has to be a God; in order for one to revolt,
there has to be an authority to rise up against. When boundaries are
blurred and values are lost, when God dies without leaving an heir, then
heroism disappears from evil, which is henceforth no longer the spur
to bold resistance or self-destruction. Nothing remains but emptiness
and pain.

Looking at the consequences of my action, I was indeed overcome with a sense of emptiness and shame. I felt no pride, no liberation. I did not love evil in itself. I had acted without feeling any pleasure, be it ever so ephemeral and illusory. There was only emptiness
and shame. Yet my vandalism was more repugnant than a senseless
theft of pears. Augustine had chosen a relatively trivial anecdote, a story
without real victims. Of course theft is reprehensible, but it is difficult
to believe that Augustine's neighbors would have missed their un-
shapely and tasteless pears. If they'd been asked for permission, they
probably would have let Augustine and his comrades gather pears to
their hearts' content. I, in contrast, had harmed somebody: I had
harmed Micky. Though we weren't friends, he'd never done me any
harm. Though he didn't know who'd hurt him, he was surely hurt.

The Bishop of Hippo, too, felt that someone had been wronged by
his act—not the owners of the pear tree, but God. Yet we can suppose

that God suffered less from Augustine's theft than Micky suffered from the destruction of his miniature city. After all, God Himself has been known to destroy cities from time to time. To the best of my recollection, I had never mistreated Micky until then. Why, then, did I do it? I don't know. Perhaps I wanted to feel that I could be, if only for a moment, an abuser rather than one of the abused. Perhaps I wanted to feel the sensation of arbitrary power, the capacity to harm without being accountable. When Sir Edmund Hillary was asked why he had climbed Mount Everest, he replied: "Because it was there." Why had I destroyed Micky's miniature city? Because it was there—because Sir Edmund and I had the power to carry out our will. I am ashamed of this tale precisely because the idiotic wickedness that it relates is uninspired, because I was exercising force without pleasure. I could have thought of many forbidden ways to procure *some* pleasure. I could have stolen things I desired, bought sexual pleasure, taken vengeance on my enemies.

I did none of that. If this story has haunted me for so many years, it is probably because it reaffirms what Augustine asserts—that the predisposition to make others suffer, to destroy, is an integral part of our nature; because undoubtedly I continue to destroy cities along my path, obeying some internal proclivity to do wrong; because even if I think my intentions are good, I might be to another person what my tormenters were to me.

Can one separate, as I did, pleasure from morality? Is it permissible to enjoy forbidden fruit? Is it possible to enjoy fruit that is *not* forbidden? How do we strike a balance between the desire to always do what we want and the price that such freedom exacts from others? The answers human societies give to these questions determine their character and make them what they are. These answers do not result only from rational discussions. They are formulated and reformulated according to needs, tendencies, and the accidents of history, according to good actions of which we are proud and villainies of which we are ashamed. This book deals with these questions. It considers the varieties of sin, the multifarious nature of guilt, and the endless cunning of self-justification.

There is no impersonal writing on sin. I've begun by speaking of myself. It is no accident that I chose to relate my sin against Micky, just as it was no accident that Augustine chose to relate how he stole worthless pears. There are species of lizards that have evolved a unique survival mechanism: they can sever their tails when they are in danger. The abandoned tail will ideally distract the attention of pursuers, who sink their teeth into the appetizer and let the main course get away. I am ashamed of my transgression, just as Augustine was ashamed of his. But each of us—each of you, dear readers—hides fouler skeletons in our closets. We confess occasionally, but we prefer not to divulge our truly shameful tales. The human restaurant serves mostly tails. But the reader who is willing to examine the writhing tail carefully, without rushing to sink his teeth into it, will learn many things about the body from which it was detached.

2

SIN FOR BEGINNERS

Christianity is founded on sin. Not that its founders were sinners; on the contrary, they seem to have been upright men. But sin is the foundation of the Christian worldview. The Christian is first and foremost a sinner, and Christianity constitutes above all the remedy for sin. Remove sin, and Christianity loses its whole *raison d'être*. Of course, the Christian God did create the world, make the earth fertile, and suspend the heavenly bodies. But all that was only the preamble and stage design for the great drama of sin and redemption. The perfection of the world, described by God himself on the sixth day as "very good,"[1] is merely the backdrop for the cosmic catastrophe brought about by the Fall of Adam and Eve.

The Ass and the Snail

In a perfect world, change can only be for the worse. Christian theologians understood this. For them, perfection inhered in the big picture, not in the details. The world from its very creation was designed to include transformation. Growth and withering were part of the divine program.[2] Wheat germ, for example, is wheat that has not yet reached its full maturity, just as dried-up straw is wheat that is past its maturity. The "before" and "after" states of wheat are imperfect compared with mature healthy wheat. Yet if one considers not a particular moment in the growth cycle but the cycle as a whole, then states of "before" and "after" are not tainted with any defect. Each stage plays a role in making the whole beautiful, rich, and dynamic, with its cycles of growth and decay, its enormous variety, its shades of light and darkness.

In antiquity, the ass represented a superior level of existence when compared with the snail, just as rational man was considered superior to irrational animals. Still, we cannot reproach God for not having created a world entirely composed of superior beings. A monotonous universe does not reflect God's sumptuous power as effectively as a world that is rich in variety and nuance. The ass is inferior to man, who is himself inferior to angels. But a universe that includes asses, humans, and angels is better than a world composed solely of angels—so long as the ass does not aspire to be human, and the angel does not lower itself to the level of man.[3] From a God's-eye view, the big picture of the world—with its light and shadows, its greater and lesser luminaries,[4] its honey and gall—is indeed "very good."

In the parts of the universe inhabited by living creatures, change is the rule. Things metamorphose. Certain creatures expire and are replaced by others; others evolve; the weak give way to the strong; the vanquished disappear into the victors. The world is in a perpetual state of flux. We cannot see the full beauty of this process because our limitations confine us to a particular time and place within this world, making it difficult for us to grasp the whole. But God, who has no such limitations, does grasp the totality of things. He can perceive a structure of order and beauty where we see only a mixture of the good and bad. Indeed, He sees beauty even when we see nothing but ugliness.[5]

What spoils this beautiful picture is the moral sphere. The Christian God is not ready to accept moral imperfection. Each sin, even if useful, arouses the Almighty's righteous anger. Consider, in the Christian economy of salvation, the most dramatic example of a useful sin: that of Judas Iscariot. Judas was a vital instrument for the redemption of mankind. Without him, where would we all be? The recently discovered Gospel of Judas portrays him as the beloved disciple, the noble collaborator of Christ. But in the canonical Gospels Judas is neither beloved nor noble. During the Last Supper, Jesus addresses his disciples, declaring that one of them will betray Him. The disciples, deeply saddened, wonder who the traitor might be. Then Jesus says to them: "The one who has dipped his hand into the bowl with me will betray me. The Son of Man will go, just as it is written about him. But woe to that man who betrays the Son of Man! It would be better for him if he had not been born."[6] The Son of Man must go, just as it is written about Him, and someone must betray Him. But the betrayer, who is acting in accordance with God's invincible will, carries full responsibility for his act. In other words, even if Jesus must die to rectify what Adam and Eve have corrupted, those responsible for his necessary death will be no less severely punished for it.

But why? Haven't they made their contribution to the beauty of the world, like the decaying wheat and the humble snail? Yes and no. Yes, for without Judas Iscariot the human race would not have been saved; no, for—unlike the snail and wheat stalk—a man does not act without consciousness or choice. He is a reasonable creature, endowed, much to his detriment, with free will. The deeds of Judas and Pontius Pilate had laudable results, but their intentions were anything but praiseworthy. If Judas had betrayed Christ in order to hasten the redemption of mankind, one could rightly wonder about the reason for his punishment. But Judas did not perform this act for the greater glory of God. He did good with the intention of doing evil. And just as a man does not bear moral responsibility for an evil act committed inadvertently, so he is not worthy of reward for a good deed performed unintentionally.

This explanation, however, has its limits. If there is to be true moral responsibility, there must be truly free will. But do we really have free will? Can we attribute free choice to a creature lacking divine perfection and subject by his very imperfection to the invisible force of circumstances? To make moral decisions, a person needs acute powers of discernment that not everyone possesses; he needs a well-tempered character allowing him to act on his moral decisions; he needs circumstances in which terror and passion do not cloud his mind. A man who makes the right moral decisions because of his genes, his character, his education, the vagaries of his life, and the goals he has set himself should consider himself lucky. Unfortunately, most of us lack such moral luck. Too many things can, and do, go wrong. Moral systems are by nature chaotic: they are both deterministic and unpredictable. According to chaos theory, a butterfly fanning its wings in Brazil can set off a chain of events resulting in a hurricane in Florida. At the beginning of this chain, one can interrupt the progression with relative ease. Yet in the early stages it is practically impossible to foresee the consequences of trivial everyday acts; it is practically impossible to foresee the hurricane in the beating of butterfly wings. In later stages, when the consequences are already foreseeable, it becomes equally impossible to arrest the process. The ultimate causes of our acts are situated in the distant past. We act as we do because this is how we have been raised, in specific circumstances largely beyond our control. We are raised by parents who bequeath us a specific genetic inheritance, and by teachers who educate us in ways shaped by the vast impersonal forces of fate and history. In the final analysis, nobody is the master of his or her acts. We are all little hurricanes that started in that distant moment when the cosmic butterfly first beat its wings.

A Relative Freedom

Saint Paul was deeply aware of this. He identifies the first couple as point zero, from which all the rest flows. Adam and Eve had neither parents nor education. They were created as perfect as possible for creatures endowed with body, soul, and mind. Their decision to sin was made in the most ideal of circumstances, in Paradise itself. Everything was quite wonderful in the Garden of Eden—but circumstances soon deteriorated considerably. From the moment original sin was committed, the question of free will lost its pertinence. Human will was irrevocably perverted.[7] The attraction toward evil was now part of our selves, as natural to us as our organs. Evil is interior; it is part of us, not an invading external agent. To be the descendant of Adam and Eve, to be human, means wishing for what is evil in the eyes of the Lord. We are weighed down by the terrible burden of original sin, a burden to which we daily add our own evil inclinations. No one is free. Even newborn babies are tainted by original sin.[8] Heirs of irresponsible parents, the children of men are born debtors in the divine moral banking system. They have no chance of erasing this debt on their own. Worse, they are totally incapable of ever producing moral income. In their account there are no deposits, only withdrawals: a monstrous and ever-growing moral debt. Remember Augustine's pear tree? Its evil roots extend back to the Garden of Eden. The soul cannot help yearning for sin. "For what I do," writes Saint Paul, "is not the good I want to do; no, the evil I do not want to do—this I keep on doing."[9]

Human beings cannot do otherwise. We are, in the most profound sense, victims of circumstances. Are we morally off the hook, then? In human terms the answer is no. In an earthly court, a man cannot plead that his cultural, psychological, and genetic heritage led him to act as he did, or that it's all the fault of some prehistoric butterfly. Courts have a short attention span. They have little patience for Brazilian butterflies and are willing to consider attenuating circumstances only when these would be recognizable to the "common sense" of the "average man." They will consider nothing that's too complicated or too far removed. Can an unbearable provocation cause an uncontrollable explosion? Can severe physical abuse transform a child into a psychopath? More complex situations are not taken into account. My parents' relationship, my character, my physique, the national culture within which I acted—all this usually has no place in the courtroom. The judge is not in a position to know whether the events of my childhood have really "made me do it" or are just an excuse. He sees only the acceptable evidence brought before him. He never sees the big picture. He is not God.

But God *is* God. He who tests hearts and minds is not reduced to judging by appearances, nor does he depend on human testimony—a *medium fallibile* ("unreliable means"), as medieval lawyers were quick to note.[10] Human judges (fallible mediums themselves) are forced to decide according to how things appear to them. Unlike human eyes, the Creator's vision perceives each hidden recess, each secret connection, the past, present, and future very clearly. From the divine point of view, no man is responsible for his acts, since no man has complete mastery over his decisions and actions. Real freedom is the privilege of the Almighty. The limited creature, a plaything of circumstances beyond its control, is not free. In retrospect, even the freedom of Adam and Eve in Paradise before the Fall was quite relative. They were free compared to us—their bodies sturdier, their intellect stronger, their will untarnished. But in relation to the perfect God, they were nothing but imperfect, fragile vessels. Sooner or later they would have fallen. If they'd been perfect, they would not have had the ability to do wrong, just as God *cannot* do wrong. He does not refrain from doing wrong because He is in any way limited. On the contrary, His freedom consists in the fact that going astray, under any circumstances, is inconsistent with His essence.

But man? Flesh and blood? Saint Paul understood that ascribing freedom to man is absurd. Indeed, such freedom would detract from the dignity of God's omnipotence. The rewards and punishments he metes out are not responses to any creature's choices, but expressions of His sovereign will. This is why Paul writes in his Letter to the Romans:

> Yet before the twins [of Rebekah] were born or had done anything good or bad—in order that God's purpose in election might stand: not by works but by him who calls—she was told, "The older will serve the younger." Just as it is written: "Jacob I loved, but Esau I hated." What then shall we say? Is God unjust? Not at all! For he says to Moses, "I will have mercy on whom I have mercy, and I will have compassion on whom I have compassion." It does not, therefore, depend on man's desire or effort, but on God's mercy. For the Scripture says to Pharaoh: "I raised you up for this very purpose, that I might display my power in you and that my name might be proclaimed in all the earth." Therefore God has mercy on whom he wants to have mercy, and he hardens whom he wants to harden. One of you will say to me: "Then why does God still blame us? For who resists his will?" But who are you, O man, to talk back to God? Shall what is formed say to him who formed it, "Why did you make me like this?" Does not the potter have the right to make out of the same lump of clay some pottery for noble purposes and some for common use?[11]

One could have given other explanations for Pharaoh's hardened heart or the preference given to Jacob over Esau. One could have argued that Esau lost his birthright by his own free choice, and that Pharaoh's stubborn pride was not the cause of his punishment but the first stage of it. Paul does not make such arguments. Centuries later, Moses Maimonides assures us in the treatise "Eight Chapters," the introduction to his commentaries on the *Pirke Avot* (Chapters of the Fathers), that there is nothing arbitrary about God's actions:

> If Pharaoh and his followers had committed no other sin than not letting Israel go free, the matter would undoubtedly be problematic, for He had prevented them from setting Israel free. As He said: *For I hardened his heart and the heart of his servants* (Exodus 10:1). Then He required that [Pharaoh] set them free, though he was compelled not to set them free. Then He punished him and destroyed him and his followers for not setting them free. This would have been an injustice and contrary to everything we have previously set forth.
>
> However, the matter is not like this, but rather Pharaoh and his followers disobeyed by choice, without force or compulsion. They oppressed the foreigners who were in their midst and treated them with sheer injustice. As it is clearly said: *And he said to his people: Behold the people of Israel. . . . Come let us deal shrewdly with them.* This action was due to their choice and to the evil character of their thought; there was nothing compelling them to do it. God punished them for it by preventing them from repenting, so that the punishment which His justice required would befall them. What prevented them from repentance was that they would not set [Israel] free.[12]

These answers seem to have satisfied Maimonides (although elsewhere he considered the existence of free choice in the predetermined world of physical forces and divine mandates truly a miracle beyond comprehension). But Saint Paul did not choose this path. He understood that such explanations merely push back the difficulty without resolving it. Could Pharaoh and his followers act against the divine plans "without force or compulsion"? Surely not. Nothing "in the world that He created according to His will"[13] is without force or compulsion. If sin exists in the world, it is because God wants it so. And why does He want it so? This is not clear. Who are we to question the Lord? Besides, what matters here is not the obscure answer (all answers to this question are obscure), but the manifest consequences of this divine decision: fallen humanity has forever lost its moral standing. From birth, we are guilty by definition. Whatever we enjoy upon this earth—including life itself—is undeserved, ill-gotten. We fill our mouths with God's forbidden fruits and render Him evil in return for good.

What God Calls Justice

What is the meaning of this tragic state? We sin; God punishes; the sum total is a perfect zero. Well, not quite. God seems discontented with this zero-sum game. He looks at the big picture and, for His own mysterious reasons, chooses to intervene. From time to time, He decides to deposit some of His vast riches in the moral account of certain individuals, thus changing their bottom line from red to black. Why these and not others? According to Saint Paul, the righteous, the holy ones whose merits intercede for us, became so not by reason of some positive quality of their own but by divine election. Why has God elected them? Who knows? Humans certainly don't. As for those who were not chosen, the bank inflicts heavy fines on them and throws them into the eternal fires of Hell. Hell is the mechanism chosen by God to balance the moral accounts of rational creatures. Each transgression has its retribution. Minor faults (in human terms) are savagely punished; fleeting evils are undone by eternal suffering. This may look terrible to us—but then, unlike God, we do not see the big picture. Hell transforms the world into a good and beautiful place. "There is no interval of time between these two [sin and punishment]; the soul does not do what it ought not at one time, and suffer what it ought at another time. The beauty of the whole must not be impaired even for a moment; it must not contain the shame of sin without the beauty of punishment."[14]

From a divine standpoint, punishment is very beautiful. And from the standpoint of the tormented in Hell? That, of course, is another story.[15] Still, as we have seen, the story does not always end up in Hell. There are occasional happy endings—thanks to grace. Grace and love have the power to undo justice, to make the big picture less balanced than it should have been. Love is God's weakness. It is, apparently, a very powerful weakness, capable of distorting justice, of disfiguring the penal beauty of Hell. God loves humans; He loves them so much "that He gave His one and only Son that whoever believes in Him shall not perish but have eternal life."[16] By an absurd and outrageous act, God defiled himself with humanity to save His creatures from His own wrath. He bent the rules of justice that He Himself had established and repaired man's corruption by a blatant breach of justice. We will come back to this. For the time being, let us ponder Saint Augustine's ambivalence in his words on divine grace and justice: "When this punishment is remitted for those who turn to him, there is great goodness [bonitas] on the part of God, and, when the due punishment is exacted, there is no injustice on the part of God. For it is better that a nature may be set in order so that it may grieve in punishment rather than rejoice with impunity in sin."[17]

Grace is goodness; it is not justice. It is just to punish the wicked—this makes the world a better place. The feeling that divine grace violates justice in the world was not invented by Christian theologians. It lies behind one of the most marvelous books of the Bible, the Book of Jonah. The author does not raise the more common dilemma of Job and the Prophets—Why do the innocent suffer?—but poses the inverse question: Why are the guilty pardoned? Jonah is sent to the great city of

Nineveh to inform its inhabitants that, in punishment for their sins, they face destruction in forty days. But the inhabitants of Nineveh repent, and God spares them and their city. At this, "Jonah is greatly displeased and becomes angry. He prays to the Lord, 'O Lord, is this not what I said when I was still at home? That is why I was so quick to flee to Tarshish. I knew that you are a gracious and compassionate God, slow to anger and abounding in love, a God who relents from sending calamity. Now, O Lord, take away my life, for it is better for me to die than to live.'"[18] Jonah is irritated at God's injustice. He refuses to live in a world without justice, where the judgments of the sovereign master of the universe are arbitrary. In the Book of Jonah, God appears out of character: not only is He not fixated on the beauty of punishment, but He is more humane than His prophet. God grows a plant to protect the angry prophet's head from the sun, then raises up a worm to chew the roots of the plant that is shading him. Human (and animal) life, says Jonah's God, are more important than abstract ideas like justice or the irate prophet's dignity: "But the Lord said, 'You have had pity on the plant for which you have not labored, nor made it grow, which came up in a night and perished in a night. And should I not pity Nineveh, that great city, in which are more than one hundred and twenty thousand people who cannot discern between their right hand and their left, and also much livestock?'"[19]

The problem with this compassionate God who spares Nineveh is that there are many cities He does not spare, just as I did not spare Micky's little city. But in God's case, the consequences are more dire. Most cities on the verge of destruction do not receive any warning or a second chance from Him. Quite often, human beings are punished—justly, of course, since they are by definition sinners—without ever fully understanding what befell them and why. In the Book of Job, Eliphaz of Teman has a revelation where he expresses in powerful words the divine conception of justice, in the face of which human justice crumbles to pieces:

> Can a mortal be more righteous than God?
> Can a man be more pure than his Maker?
> If God places no trust in his servants,
> If he charges his angels with error,
> How much more those who live in houses of clay,
> Whose foundations are in the dust,
> Who are crushed more readily than a moth!
> Between dawn and dusk they are broken into pieces;
> Unnoticed, they perish forever.
> Are not the cords of their tent pulled up,
> So that they die without wisdom?[20]

God puts no trust even in his servants. He finds fault with the angels. How much more blameworthy are humans, whose bodies are made of clay, who are crushed more easily than moths, who perish unnoticed, without understanding? They die without knowing wherefore or why. And this is what God calls justice. For in its most terrible manifestations, justice is merely a synonym for the divine will. Justice is what God wants. What God does in His might is right by definition. Unlike God, men cannot always be right. Like the blind in an unknown city, they try to find their way to their maker's path, to find grace in His ever-observing eyes. In vain. "God places no trust in his servants and charges his angels with error!" But isn't this Job's complaint to God? Not that He punishes the innocent, as the prophets continually object, but that his absolute powers and absolute justice render human justice impossible:

> Man born of woman is of few days and full of trouble.
> He springs up like a flower and withers away;
> Like a fleeting shadow, he does not endure.
> Do you fix your eye on such a one?
> Will you bring him before you for judgment?

Who can bring what is pure from the impure?
No one![21]

God can of course bring what is pure from the impure. In theory, God could have undone Adam and Eve's deed. He could have canceled the debts of humans by a simple act of divine will, since nothing is impossible for God. But He did not choose this path. The Jewish God simply lowers His expectations. He is willing to be satisfied with the relative righteousness of humans and to judge them in terms of a relative justice that they can understand and act upon. We promise to obey His commandments and He promises to exercise leniency, to be clement, to turn a blind eye to our errors and imperfections and let us live a little longer in our houses of clay with their dusty foundations.

But Paul's God would not turn a blind eye. To avoid His justice from exploding and throwing all of humanity into Hell, God must somehow derail His passion for justice.[22] Justice demands sacrifices. Suffering satisfies that demand. But whose suffering? Human suffering does not stop the man-eating mechanism of God's justice. The only thing capable of bringing it to a halt is an act of scandalous injustice, a divine outrage so horrific that the wheels of divine justice will allow at least some human beings to escape unpunished. What could constitute such a holy outrage? God chose to become man and sacrifice Himself. He became the perfect scapegoat, the Lamb of God whose blood can wash away human sins: Jesus Christ, God incarnate. Bearing our sins, assuming our tainted flesh, He let pity replace justice. How wonderful! "O happy fault [*felix culpa*] that merited such and so great a redeemer!"[23] sings the Church in the ceremony of lighting the Easter candles. If one looks carefully, one can perhaps see through the candle smoke a flash of pride in the eyes of Adam and Eve. Without them— without original sin, that happy fault—we would not enjoy this magnificent blessing, the greatest miracle of humanity: the descent to earth of the Lord of Heaven. "How you have fallen from heaven, O morning star, son of the dawn! You have been cast down to the earth, you who once laid low the nations!"[24] If they did not succeed in being like God, they at least succeeded in making God into a man.

It is terrible to be a man. For God, who is not used to it, it was a thousand times more terrible. Humiliated and tortured, pierced and left bleeding upon the Cross, He breathed his last with a heartbreaking cry: "My God, my God, why have you forsaken me?"[25] The death of Christ on the Cross is such a horrible injustice—the absolutely unjust death of the one absolutely innocent being—that the glow of the just flames of Hell loses its beauty.

Everything becomes absurd after the Crucifixion. Men are saved through a sin immeasurably worse than original sin: the murder of God. This act adds a horrible stain to man's conscience, even while re-deeming humanity. Why doesn't the murder of God require a punishment more terrible than the sin of having tasted the forbidden fruit? Why, instead of crying from the ground,[26] does God's blood wash and purify sinners? Is this not unjust? Does it not defy human reason? Exactly, observes Saint Paul:

> The message of the Cross is foolishness to those who are perishing; but to us who are being saved, it is the power of God. For it is written: "I will destroy the wisdom of the wise; the intelligence of the intelligent I will frustrate."
>
> Where is the wise man? Where is the scholar? Where is the philosopher of this age? Has not God made foolish the wisdom of the world? For since in the wisdom of God the world through its wisdom did not know him, God was pleased through the foolishness of what was preached to save those who believe. Jews demand miraculous signs and Greeks look for wisdom, but we preach Christ crucified, a

stumbling block to Jews and foolishness to Gentiles; but to those whom God has called, both Jews and Greeks, Christ is the power of God and the wisdom of God. For the foolishness of God is wiser than man's wisdom, and the weakness of God is stronger than man's strength.

Brothers, think of what you were when you were called. Not many of you were wise by human standards; not many were influential; not many were of noble birth. But God chose the foolish things of the world to shame the wise; God chose the weak things of the world to shame the strong. He chose the lowly things of this world and the despised things—and the things that are not—to nullify the things that are, so that no one may boast before him.[27]

In fact, nobody can boast before Paul's God. Absolute inequality characterizes the relations between God and His faithful. The rules of divine grace are beyond human understanding. The justice of divine *quid pro quo*—cruel but comprehensible—has been deliberately destroyed by God on the Cross. But the divine act of generosity paralyzes the faithful. What can the believer say? That God did not do enough for men? Had He not been made flesh and died on the Cross for us and for our salvation? Can those who were not chosen for salvation reproach Him who had washed sinners with His innocent blood?

Insurance Policy against Hell

Herein lies a great difference between Judaism and Christianity. For the Jew, it is indeed God who established the rules of the game (justice); and, since He is Almighty, nobody can hold Him accountable. But—at least with respect to His chosen people—God cannot act according to the rules of His incomprehensible justice. God has willingly chosen to subject Himself to the terms of a contract, the Covenant, with the Jewish people. This Covenant consists of precise clauses that are accessible to the human mind and that bind God and His chosen people equally. It is impossible to compel God to behave according to the rules of this contractual justice, but one can waive the contract and reprimand God: "Will not the Judge of all the earth do right?"[28] Moreover, even if Judaism recognizes the limits of human capacities, it does not imagine God imposing rules that His people would be unable to obey. Nor can God expect *perfect* execution of His precepts with pure and total commitment. Total commitment is extremely rare in a world where humans are torn between *yetser ha-tov* ("good inclination") and *yetser ha-ra* ("evil inclination"). The created world is by nature imperfect. Moral perfection is unique to God, and moral excellence is rare. Salvation is about being good enough. According to Judaism, people accumulate points (good deeds) during their lives. Those who have accumulated enough points are saved. It's that simple.

In Pauline Christianity, there is no accumulation of points. Even after the death of Jesus on the Cross, the human aptitude to do good is not restored. Without grace, we are lost. Those who are saved, a small minority really, are saved thanks to election and not on their own merits. If grace were granted in exchange for works (human actions or effort), it would no longer be grace but would be simply wages. Grace, writes Saint Augustine of Hippo—Saint Paul's greatest interpreter— must be *gratis* or it would not be grace. God owes us nothing. We are all guilty. There are no righteous people—only evildoers who have been pardoned.

The Pauline-Augustinian view of salvation and grace constitutes a veritable revolution in religious thought. It detaches ethics from reward and punishment. A person must do good without any certainty that God will recompense him for his actions or intentions. God may choose to save His worst enemies (Paul felt he was one of them, when God's grace threw him off his horse on the road to Damascus) and to damn His most devoted followers (Judas, after all, was one of the twelve Apostles). Appearances are nothing. Common sense is nothing. God's will is everything. "Shall what is formed say to him who formed it, 'Why did you make me like this?' Does not the potter have the right to make out of the same lump of clay some pottery for noble purposes and some for common use?"[29] Religion ceases to be a certificate of guarantee ("Seek me and live")[30] and becomes an act that is truly heroic (Seek me even if you will not live).

How many of us can choose good for its own sake, knowing that after a life of devotion and piety we may end up in Hell? Be honest—not very many. The Church was not content with the few. It did not call itself Catholic (meaning "universal") for nothing. It wanted the masses; it wanted the entire world. It aimed at the lowest common psychological denominator: the unheroic fear of punishment, not heroic faith.[31] Only a handful of individuals are free of this fear; only a handful are capable of faith for faith's sake. Without fear, people would swallow each other alive.[32] Without the fear of God, the Church would be only a small group of powerless enthusiasts. One soon gets bored with being powerless.

As soon as the clergy convinced enough people that it possessed the keys to the Kingdom of Heaven, the right to decide here below who will enter the gates of Paradise and who will be thrown into the eternal flames of Hell, the Church became important. In earthly terms, the Church may not be very powerful. But our earthly existence passes quickly, and then we have an eternity of otherworldly life ahead of us.[33] For one must never forget—and one is often reminded—that despite God's meekness during His earthly sojourn, He is prone to vengeance. Vengeance is mine, said the Lord. He will demand accounts from those who disrespected His Church. Are you planning to aggravate the holders of the keys? Think again. "Woe to you who are well fed now, for you will go hungry. Woe to you who laugh now, for you will mourn and weep."[34]

Is this traditional idea of an ethics of exchange (be good to God and He'll be good to you) consistent with Paul's theology of grace? Not really. What does one do, then? One seeks compromises. Nobody would dream of contesting the authority of Saint Paul; but his ideas were very difficult to understand. They had to be interpreted so they would not transform the simple believer into a fatalist doing whatever seemed good to him while hoping for grace. Without the fear of authority, as we know, God alone knows what people are capable of doing. The Church thus chose to offer ordinary believers a theology that stresses the preponderant importance of grace, while elegantly turning it into a specific kind of remuneration. Without divine grace, nobody would be saved, but this grace is not distributed in an arbitrary fashion; to a certain extent, it is granted to the whole human race as a theoretical possibility of redemption (which would not have existed without Christ's sacrifice). But this potentiality does not suffice to win a person entry into the Kingdom of Heaven. For *that,* one has to work. Grace is more generously granted to the person who works—that is, to the one who does the will of the Lord and His representatives on earth. Thus, the Church succeeded (well, more or less, as we shall see) in having its cake (grace) and eating it (works).

Once it was established that a Christian could affect his or her destiny—even if this influence was dependent on the collaboration of God's grace—a systematic examination of sin became essential. Even for Saint Paul, a community committed to his idea of grace must distinguish between sinners and nonsinners (whatever their status in the eyes of God). But too much attention to the fine legal points of our do's and don't's is superfluous. It is too Jewish. Saint Paul pronounces both Jewish law and Jewish legalism null and void. If only faith, hope, and love matter—faith in Christ, hope in His salvation, love of God and neighbor—then the rest is secondary and relatively unimportant. But if human actions, sins, and good deeds do determine the destiny of the believer, then it is vital to discuss them.

In the ancient world, the philosophical discussion of virtue (*aretē* in Greek, *virtus* in Latin) was much more widespread than any debate over vice. *Aretē* is moral excellence; it expresses what is best in men; the person endowed with this quality makes the most of human potential. Vices are associated with various sorts of misunderstanding and error, provoked by carnal passions and instincts. The reasonable man uses reason to resist the Siren song of the passions and succeeds in living as a man should. The fool is controlled by his passions and lives like an animal.[35]

For Christians, something more significant than self-fulfillment was placed on the balance. To do good did not bring human potential to fruition, the way the wheat germ becomes the fully grown sheaf of wheat. The potential for spiritual growth was destroyed by Adam and Eve's sin, and too much concern with perfecting the self was seen by Christian theologians as pernicious for the soul. No, virtue was less about self-fulfillment and more about self-preservation. Virtue was an insurance policy against Hell. The best of virtues was obedience to God's will. You could not do wrong so long as you obeyed His commandments without qualm or objection. Vice was no longer both crime *and* punishment, as the Greek philosophers thought (since vice is irrational, giving in to it entailed a deformation of the rational soul, and the philosophers could imagine no greater evil). For the theologians, moral transgressions were not their own punishment. They were not a psychological problem, but a legal one. The Almighty's court was always in session, and His eternal torture chambers never closed. Like the rabbis, however, Church leaders developed a rather realistic view of human moral abilities. Moral excellence was destined for the very few; Hell was a very realistic possibility for everyone else.

The Ecclesiastical Shortlist of Sins

"Sin lies at the door," God warned Cain.[36] But not all sins are the same. Let us begin with the basic categories that the Church's experts devised. First of all, there is original sin *(peccatum originale)* inherited from Adam and Eve. Sin is in our nature, not in our nurture, and it can be washed away only by the baptism of water or the baptism of blood (dying for the faith). Then, there is venial sin *(peccatum veniale)*, erased by confession and an act of contrition before a priest. Finally, there is mortal sin *(peccatum mortale)*. A mortal sin destroys the soul and blocks the action of grace. Unless it is purified by deep repentance and absolved by a person with the authority to grant absolution for that particular offense, a mortal sin condemns the sinner's soul to Hell. Certain mortal sins are so grave that only a bishop, or in some cases the pope, can absolve them. Christian theologians spilled oceans of ink over these distinctions in the most minute and exhaustive detail.

What is right and what is wrong? What can be pardoned and what is unforgivable? Every culture must deal with these questions.[37] Our moral code is an attempt to answer them. But behind our moral codes and our law books lurks a whole array of hidden assumptions— assumptions about human psychology, about the nature of God, about the structure of society, about gender difference and social stratification, about hope and despair. This book mostly deals with what precedes formal judgment. In other words, it deals with cultural prejudices. It looks at the vices—those nuclear reactors of passion that explode into sin. The passion to do what is good in our own eyes rather than in His eyes resides in the soul of every human being. One must always be on guard. Sin waits at the door. If the traveler does not carefully examine the moral maps provided by religion, he is not likely to return to the heavenly home safely.

The Catholic Church has counted seven vices, super-sins that give birth to a host of others. These are known as the seven deadly sins.

The concept of a Christian shortlist of sins made its appearance in the first centuries after Christ. In the fourth century, the monk Evagrius Ponticus drew up a list of eight "capital" sins.[38] His disciple John Cassian, who emigrated from Egypt and founded a monastery in Marseille, helped to spread the idea in the West.[39] At the start of the fifth century, the Spanish writer Prudentius composed a poem entitled *Psychomachia* (The Battle of the Soul) that describes not eight but seven deadly sins.[40] The number seven enchanted the people of antiquity, and when a list of sins assumed sufficient importance, it quite naturally was poured into the mold of a number greatly appreciated at that time. Prudentius describes the virtues and vices as women fighting each other in a series of duels to the death. His poem had immense success among ecclesiastics, and the number of sins was henceforth fixed at seven.[41]

What are they? Opinions varied. For Prudentius, they were idolatry, discord, lust, anger, pride, vanity, and greed. The so-called Last of the Church Fathers, Pope Gregory the Great (540–604), discusses the capital sins in his influential *Morals on the Book of Job*. He cites a verse from Ecclesiasticus (10:15) affirming that "pride is the source [*initium*] of all sins."[42] Hence, according to Saint Gregory, pride is not a specific sin but an instinct that forms the basis of all sins. The seven on his shortlist are vanity, envy, anger, despair (moral sloth), greed, gluttony, and lust. In the course of time, vanity and pride were blended into a single sin.[43] Thus was established in the West the traditional list of the seven capital sins.[44]

This book does not deal with the historical vicissitudes of the vices, nor with the discussions of theologians who tried to make sense of the deadly sins. Nor does it deal systematically with the sudden disappearance of sin from the cultural scene in the modern era. Since the end of the twentieth century, sin as a living presence has gone out of fashion in the West.[45] Even men of the Church now tend to psychologize sin and rarely refer to it as a legal offense that would send a person to Hell. Hell, too, is definitely out. These are important issues, and great volumes have been devoted to them. What I offer the reader here is something else: a slim volume, an essay on the human passions, a personal look at the impulses that make our lives wonderful or horrible, or both.

In the ancient tradition of Jewish writing, one avoids saying too much. No statement is ever definitive. Reading is not a passive process of absorption, but a trigger. The author should let the reader "complete the sentences." In the academic tradition, on the other hand, one always tries to be definitive, exhaustive, to have the last word—or many last words. In this book, I have chosen the older of these traditions.

SLOTH
Acedia

Sloth is not the worst of the deadly sins. If I begin with it, it is because sloth is the vice I must overcome at the moment. The Latin word *acedia* (or *acidia*) is derived from the Greek *akēdēs,* meaning "indifferent," "careless."[1] Some people detest work and *enjoy* idleness. That's outrageous. God hates them.[2] He expects hard work. The Latin *cultus Dei* and the Hebrew *avodat Elohim* both mean "the labor of God." But sloth is not only aversion to work. It may also signify despair, despair at the Sisyphean labor and ephemeral reward that are the lot of those who work hard. In the Middle Ages, the person who committed suicide, who preferred the total absence of action to the hard work of penance and reingratiation, was a common symbol of *acedia.* The man who lost hope was idle not for the pleasure of idleness, but because he became spiritually indifferent. Since all was lost, there was no point in trying to shake off sin. One might as well shorten the suffering. It is this indifference that constitutes the sin of spiritual sloth.[3] "Even when a sharp sword rests upon a man's throat, he should not despair of [God's] mercy."[4] Even Judas Iscariot ought to have put his hope in God and His Son, for whom nothing is impossible. Even the traitor *par excellence* could have been saved. Idleness will kill you.

There are, then, two kinds of sloth: optimistic sloth, which shuns work for more agreeable occupations,[5] and pessimistic sloth, which abstains from action for want of confidence or through despair.[6] This division of sloth reflects the social division of labor. The slothful factory worker wonders, as in Jacques Prévert's famous poem "Le Temps perdu" (A Waste of Time), whether it's a good idea to give a perfectly beautiful day to the boss; the slothful intellectual wonders if beautiful days have any point and whether writing books is really worth the trouble. Writing a book entails confronting both kinds of sloth. I sit down in front of my computer and immediately I discover the fascinating beauty of the world. Everything—except writing—attracts my eyes and my mind. I yearn to read books which I haven't glanced at for years—to finally finish reading Karl Marx's *Das Kapital.* I avidly skim newspaper editorials, rush with great eagerness to answer the telephone; I dedicate myself to preparing the perfect cup of coffee and to meticulously sorting my papers. I try to fix household appliances (with little success). Anyone trying to help me devote myself to writing provokes an anger that I am, of course, obliged to hide. At such moments, I must admit, I prefer anything to writing.

But not writing is more than a simple shirking of work, a failure to meet deadlines and comply with a contract. It also means confronting the more fearsome forces of self-doubt. The page that won't be filled calls into question my industry and my sense of responsibility. But this isn't the real problem. The blank page is simultaneously evidence for the prosecution and star witness for the defense. So long as it is empty, it constitutes irrefutable proof of my incapacity. But so long as I do not cover it with words, it also serves as my alibi. In Latin, *alibi* means "elsewhere" or "not here." So long as the page remains empty, it could be filled with all kinds of things. Had I not been prevented by those damn phone calls and by the urgent need to read *Das Kapital,* I just might have filled it, in a fabulous rush of creativity, with words of wisdom and beauty. The unwritten work is always better than the written one. The difference between the unwritten and the written, as Aristotle explains in his *Poetics,* is like the difference between poetry and history. Poetry is about what would, could, or should have been; history is merely the description of what Alcibiades did and what others did to him.[7] What I have *not* written is potentially perfect. What I have *in fact* written is what was written by Aviad Kleinberg—nothing more. Writing (even when not about sin) always has an element of self-exposure. Filling the page arouses every intellectual's fear of being exposed as a phony. We dread the raised eyebrows of our fellows—"Is that all?" Deep inside, we know that there should have been more, that it should have been better. Sometimes this feeling of inadequacy causes total paralysis. Sometimes (very rarely) an author is so sure of his abilities that he does not feel this inadequacy at all. Most often, this internal struggle ends in a compromise: the decision to refer to the higher authority of the reader. "Here is what I wrote. I have not succeeded in writing anything better. Judge the result for yourselves—and pray be gentle."

The Church Fathers were quite familiar with this type of *acedia.* Most of them did not earn their bread by the sweat of their brow, but knew a thing or two about intellectual angst and spiritual melancholy. Intellectual sloth, they noted, was closely linked to another fault attributed to the literati: pride. Anybody who thinks he is in a position to write something truly worthy, would be seized with despair in the face of his own limitations. A person who despairs because he is not Shakespeare commits the sin of pride. Experienced abbots constantly ran into novices who passionately declared themselves to be the greatest sinners in the world. The exasperated abbot had to rebuke those monks for their arrogance. The greatest of sinners? Only someone suffering from dangerous megalomania could think that his puny sins, his miserable faults, amounted to absolute evil. Very probably, such a greenhorn enthusiast was just a mediocre sinner like the rest of us. Like the vain in general, the novice chafes against his mediocrity. He craves (unwarranted) attention—be it positive or negative. Instead of improving himself, he proclaims himself incorrigible. He should be sent to work—real, not spiritual, work. Or he should be beaten: fatigue and pain would help him to get rid of his pride and sloth. Sloth is not for the weary.

Twiddling Thumbs

While pessimistic sloth (spiritual despondency) belongs to those who have free time and high pretensions, what I have called optimistic sloth or laziness—avoiding tasks in favor of pleasure—is the sin of the working man and woman. For those who wield authority over other people's time—employers, supervisors, professors, parents—laziness has nothing positive about it. It upsets timetables, trespasses deadlines, and disrupts projects. Instead of living up to expectations, laziness simply lies down and twiddles its thumbs. At its core, this kind of laziness is a subversive act, a peculiar type of disobedience. Open rebellion stimulates the power system into action, and spurs the ruling classes to moral outrage, warlike ardor, and a thirst for blood. But sloth is a quiet revolt, without manifestos or ideology. It is social judo—"the gentle way." It obtains results by exhausting the timekeepers. Since it is both ubiquitous and low-key, sloth prevents them from mobilizing all their forces for the decisive stroke. They find it difficult to decide what to do; they become hoarse and weary. Finally they shrug their shoulders, roll their eyes, and throw away the stopwatch. Soon they will contract the very sin they are combating. Sloth is infectious.

To combat sloth, someone must always be watching. And someone, you lazy workers, is forever watching you from up above, even when the earthly bosses, supervisors, and overseers are away. Time is short and work is abundant.[8] It is essential to impress upon the workers that their laziness is harmful to themselves first and foremost. Earthly bosses do make a profit on laborers' work. But the workers themselves profit most from their labor. If not on the material level, then on the spiritual level; if not in this world, then at least in the next.

Of course, bosses work less than workers. Their bed is comfortable and their glass is full. Laborers work themselves into the ground and shiver at night. But do not be misled by these deceptive appearances. The masters are working hard, very hard, spiritually. Not everybody can perform this difficult spiritual labor. Those who are incapable should trade it for respectable manual labor. The main objective is not to fall into idleness, the mother of all the vices. Work liberates and redeems. You must not sit around doing nothing, twiddling your thumbs.

Yet, in our world of inequality, idleness can be a balancing system, a technique for economizing energy and jamming the wheels of oppression.[9] The more the worker conserves his strength, the more he reduces the gap between the hard labor required of him and the modest recompense he gets. More than once collective sloth has succeeded where open rebellion had failed. Think of the role that dodging, shirking, and economic indifference played in the downfall of the Communist empire. Millions and millions of workers got up each morning and tried to evade work and punishment, tried to do less for the socialist homeland and more for their own sake. The promises of a future paradise (proletarian or religious) are very lovely indeed. But the lazy worker tastes the promised paradise here and now. For what is paradise but eternal and unrestrained idleness? Of course, in Paradise before the Fall, man had to work: "The Lord God took the man and put him in the Garden of Eden to work it and take care of it."[10] Wasn't work the reason for Adam's revolt? Wasn't he punished with hard labor because idleness filled his head with dangerous ideas? In the postlapsarian Paradise, nobody works. There is nothing but everlasting rest there, and angelic choirs. An eternal Sabbath.

We're not there yet, but it is worth noting that in the West, people are no longer keen on condemning idleness. Most of our hard labor is done by machines or (less high-tech but just as cost effective) by poorly paid Third World workers. Contemporary Western culture devotes much energy to the agreeable pastime of making good use of its free time. Leisure is no longer the time needed for resting weary bodies, but rather "quality time." The great enemies of our lifestyle (for today we are not content with simply having a life) are no longer exhaustion and hunger, but boredom and bingeing. As a result, sloth has been rehabilitated. But entertainment has become such time-consuming, exhausting work that sometimes we need a rest from rest. The new sloth requires hard work.

As leisure spreads from the top to the bottom of Western society, so does spiritual laziness, which is no longer the vice of the upper classes. Melancholy, depression, and angst are perceived not as the inevitable consequence of idleness, but as symptoms of spiritual indigestion—nothing that an hour in the gym or a good dose of Prozac or Xanax can't cure. Those in full control of their time often suffer from a feeling that life is "sound and fury, signifying nothing," that nothing they do can stop time from inanely and vainly passing. They are forever "à la recherche du temps perdu." No matter how hard they play, they remain unsatisfied. Consider Ecclesiastes, traditionally identified as King Solomon. Upon becoming the king of Israel in Jerusalem, he commissions gardens, palaces, and fountains, acquires slaves and servants, amasses silver and gold, procures men and women singers, and possesses a harem.[11] None of these things satisfies him. On the contrary, Ecclesiastes considers everything and declares it all to be vanity, chasing after the wind:[12]

> What does man gain from all his labor at which he toils
>   under the sun?
> Generations come and generations go, but the earth
>   remains forever.

The sun rises and the sun sets, and hurries back to where it
   rises.
The wind blows to the south and turns to the north; round
   and round it goes, ever returning on its course.
All streams flow into the sea, yet the sea is never full.
To the place the streams come from, there they return
   again.
All things are wearisome, more than one can say.
The eye never has enough of seeing, nor the ear its fill of
   hearing.
What has been will be again,
What has been done will be done again;
There is nothing new under the sun.[13]

If all things are wearisome, what is the point of doing anything? It's
not that Ecclesiastes fails to perceive among his well-kept gardens and
his lovely fountains, his slaves and harem, the presence of injustice all
around him. He perceives it perfectly:

Again, I looked and saw all the oppression that was taking
   place under the sun:
I saw the tears of the oppressed—and they have no
   comforter;
Power was on the side of their oppressors—and they have
   no comforter.
And I declared that the dead, who had already died,
Are happier than the living, who are still alive.
But better than both is he who has not yet been, who has
   not seen the evil that is done under the sun.[14]

But injustice does not goad Ecclesiastes to action, or even to a desire
to act. The existential sloth of Ecclesiastes, his renunciation of action,

brings no joy to this son of David but fills his life with bitterness. Worse still, it leads him to become totally disgusted with life. "And I declared that the dead, who had already died, are happier than the living, who are still alive. But better than both is he who has not yet been, who has not seen the evil that is done under the sun." Even these apparently determined words do not move Ecclesiastes to act. In the final analysis, he is content with words.

Ecclesiastes is not a philosopher of action. His death wishes remain simple wishes. Instead of improving the world or leaving it voluntarily, he chooses hedonism, the earthly life—even if that, too, like all the rest, is only vanity.

It is hard to get enthusiastic about Ecclesiastes' idea of the world. It seems he himself lost the taste for enthusiasm. Rather than living, he merely exists, in desperation, resigned to the status quo. He may think that not existing would be better—but even this would require action, from which he prefers to abstain. It has often been rightly noted that Ecclesiastes is the least religious book of the Bible. God does not make his appearance until the last chapter, and then only in a postscript, almost as an afterthought. Most of the book displays a nonreligious spirit. Ecclesiastes does not talk about moral obligations, or about Providence looking down and observing the lazy workers below. If a man wakes up every morning like a rising lion to do *avodat haboreh* (the Creator's work),[15] despair will not take hold of him and the world will not seem to him empty of meaning.[16] If you ask the pious, they will tell you that faith is the only effective antidote to existential angst. Life may seem tasteless and chaotic to the unbeliever, but to those who believe, it is full of the meaning conferred upon it by the presence and will of God. Secular antidepressants have an imminent expiration date. Only *religious* Prozac really works. Work, the Lord's work—that's all it takes.

Perhaps. Must one have religious faith to give meaning to life and banish despair? I don't think so. In the final analysis, ascribing meaning to life is an individual decision to act despite the defects of life and the shortcomings of the living. One can write imperfect books. One can live one's life without lying to oneself, and without feeling that all is vanity—at least, not *all* is vanity.

Doing Good the Stoic Way

There were some who found meaning in life and in acting, without self-delusion and without trying to please a heavenly boss. The Stoics displayed an impressive capacity to resist moral paralysis and to ascribe meaning to life, even in very difficult circumstances.[17] These philosophers attached little importance to metaphysical and epistemological questions. They certainly had views on the world and on our means of perceiving it, but for them the essential question remained our capacity to be moral persons, and especially to act in a moral way in this world, with its good and its evil.

The Stoic sees himself as duty-bound to obey a system of ethical rules that offer no reward apart from the very fact of doing what is right. No paradise awaits the Stoic after death, and in life he does not expect applause or fear the catcalls of his fellow men. Doing the right thing is not about winning a popularity contest. In fact, a large part of Stoic training *(askēsis)* aims to put the man aspiring for wisdom into a state of "stoic calm"—*ataraxia* or *apatheia* (the Stoic constantly imagines moral dilemmas and rehearses in his mind the "right" solution until it becomes second nature to him). He must act out of interior serenity, not social pressure. The Stoic hero ignores the loud choruses of approval and disapproval, and listens only to the commanding inner whisper of his conscience.[18]

The Stoic is not content with doing good for his own sake. He is not content with cultivating his own garden and polishing his own soul until it shines like gold. He considers himself obliged to do good to others and for others. Unlike the Christian hermit, the Stoic moral man cannot abstain from contact with others. Removing oneself from the company of others is an egotistical, soul-destroying act. But interacting with others is not without its moral price. The dirt of action sticks to your fingers. He who acts renounces purity. He must make compromises. The Stoic knows that. He mixes with people for the good of all, since (according to Stoic philosophy) all men are brothers, citizens of the "global city" *(kosmopolis)* of the human race. For the Stoic, the world is never vanity. It is the common garden that we must cultivate, together, for human beings bear a responsibility for one another. No moral human being is a bystander. Morality is not a spectator sport.

But sometimes the moral man runs up against an evil that he cannot correct despite all his efforts. Then the Stoic sage may choose to leave the world, with no regrets or fear. He does not end his life out of despair; if that were the case, it would be a resounding failure of his worldview and of his philosophical training. His decision is the result of rational consideration. For there are circumstances where moral action is no longer possible. Only then does life become devoid of meaning—in the phrase of the Stoic philosopher Epictetus, "the room fills with smoke."[19] In order to avoid a smoke-filled life, the Stoic prefers to open the door and leave. Someone who has lived well has no need of a life after death, and the Stoic does not believe in one anyway. For him, the possibility of departing at a time of his own choosing, before life turns him into an animal, constitutes an action as moral as any other. It is man's advantage over animals.[20]

Stoic philosophy is a philosophy of action. This is why I find it so attractive. It was not a sterile intellectual exercise. Stoicism was the philosophy adopted by eminent men of action (Emperor Marcus Aurelius was an important Stoic philosopher). An ethical theory that does not call for and result in action is only empty words, leading to despair and cynicism. For me, an ideology whose goal is to do what is good *in the eyes of the Lord*, rather than what is good, is deeply immoral. It replaces a person's moral responsibility with absolute submission to a master, even if it is the master of the universe. (Like the Stoics, I think that losing your freedom of choice means losing your soul.)

Stoic philosophy is neither pose nor sophistry. I wish that, like the Stoic sages, I could accept reality such as it is, with its good and its bad sides, without yielding to bitterness; I wish I could decide to do good and walk the right path according to the choices of my conscience alone, while accepting reality such as it is. Each night, when I reflect upon the day gone by, I want to feel that I have made the world a little better. This is not the case, I fear. More than once, lying on my bed at night, I've been forced to admit that I have not made this a better world. Even worse, I have not even tried—sometimes out of egoism and out of submission to other vices (which we will consider shortly); sometimes out of weakness or cowardice. Discouraged by obstacles awaiting me on the straight and narrow path of the good, I preferred to stay home. I have surrendered my weapons, declaring in advance that the struggle was lost. Sometimes I put my hand to the plow and looked back without finishing the furrow. Sometimes I marched in the ranks. I listened too much to the Greek chorus of my spectators, even when I pretended not to be listening. Applause is balm to my soul; catcalls wound me like sword thrusts. I stagger like a drunk from one side of the right road to the other.

But I continue. The room is not yet filled with smoke. Life is not as good as it should have been and not as bad as it could have been. Every day I tell myself that inaction, despair, and fatalistic acceptance of evil are a justification for evil. I refuse to accept evil. For villains often thrive thanks to the complacency of well-wishers. We may not win the good battle, but we are obliged to do our best. No more, but no less.

Just as there are those who would not write anything that isn't a masterpiece, there are those who refuse to act unless their own and their collaborators' motivations are without stain and blemish. How do we know that we are not obeying some hidden agenda, serving our own interests, doing more damage than good? We drown in the endless whirlpools of moral doubt, of self-criticism, of endless weighing of pros and cons, while others, less scrupulous, act. In the end, moral action should be almost a reflex, like the pharyngeal or gag reflex that contracts the back of the throat to prevent something noxious from entering the body. Stopping evil can prevent moral choking.

The daily struggle against evil is a moral obligation for each of us, even if its chances of success are small. In the end, a man must do good day after day, in the smallest combats against evil. Even if these struggles often fail to end in victory, we do not have the right to renounce them. When my time comes, said the Hassidic rabbi Zousha of Anapoli (1718–1800), "they will not ask me why I was not Moses or Abraham; they ask why I was not Zousha." Our time comes every day, each time we run up against evil. When the goal is worthy, it is worth fighting—and losing—for. The daily good—to oppose evil, meanness, petty malice, to struggle against oppression, discrimination, and marginalization—is always a worthy objective. In each act of generosity, in each good daily action (human, not divine), in each saving of a single soul, a whole universe is saved.[21]

When one struggles for justice, sometimes one discovers that the cause is not lost, that the forces of evil and hatred are tired, and that a little shove is sufficient to lay them low. Do not succumb to sloth. All is not vanity.

4

ENVY
Invidia

In Saint Augustine's view, there is nothing innocent about babies. Human beings come into the world capable of all sorts of mischief. The only difference between tender newborns and hardened old sinners is in their ability to bring harmful inclinations to fruition. The latter are obviously better at this than the former. "It is the feebleness of infant limbs that is innocent, not the infant's mind," notes the Bishop of Hippo.[1] Observing these sweet creatures, he is not impressed—at least, not favorably. They may look harmless, but give them time.[2] My father was similarly skeptical. He used to hold little babies in his arms, caress their sweet heads, then turn to the parents and say: "So, has he said, 'Dad is an ass' yet? He hasn't? He will."

Being rather optimistic by nature, my father did not draw any weighty conclusions from his thoughts on intergenerational criticism. Augustine, a pessimist, did. Beyond the general observation that no son or daughter of Adam and Eve is truly innocent, he detected in young children much that he did not like in himself—ambition, pride, impatience, and envy.

> I have personally watched and studied a jealous baby. He could not yet speak and, pale with jealousy and bitterness,

glared at his brother sharing his mother's milk. Who is un-
aware of this fact of experience? Mothers and nurses claim
to charm it away by their own private remedies. But it can
hardly be innocence, when the source of milk is flowing
richly and abundantly, not to endure a share going to one's
blood-brother, who is in profound need, dependent for life
exclusively on that one food. But people smilingly tolerate
this behavior, not because it is nothing or only a trivial matter, but because with coming of age it will pass away. You
can prove this to be the case from the fact that the same
behavior cannot be borne without irritation when encoun-
tered in someone of more mature years.[3]

Augustine's sour view of infants would not have shocked his con-
temporaries. Like us, they found babies cute and harmless—but they
did not consider them little angels. Babies were little savages dominated
by uncontrolled desires and passions, savages that only a severe up-
bringing could transform into decent human beings. Of course, the
process could not start at too tender an age; this would be pointless,
since little children were irrational and could not listen to reason. But
when they had become "old enough to know better," education was
harsh and often violent. The teachers' attribute was the whip. "He who
spares the rod hates his son."[4] Augustine himself tells us in his *Confessions* that he was repeatedly beaten, often without understanding why
he was being punished.[5] What was wrong with these savage beatings, in
Augustine's view, was the fact that his teachers were worldly men who
tried to teach him worldly wisdom and inspire him with worldly ambition. Unexplained punishment per se did not bother him, since God
rarely explained why He inflicted great suffering on human beings. Appearances notwithstanding, babies were not harmless. They had inherited from Adam and Eve a stubborn will to do evil. Infants who died
unbaptized could be punished eternally for the mere accident of not

ENVY

being cleansed of original sin through baptism. The feebleness of their limbs may have prevented them from doing evil, but their evil minds were yearning to succumb to temptation.

Augustine's idea of responsibility without understanding seems objectionable to most of us today. We refuse to see babies as sinners. We do not believe that infant suffering is justified (in fact, we see it as a prime example of *injustice*) and we tend, generally, to spare the rod. But in our post-Freudian universe, we rarely see babies as passionless creatures. Freud may have dismissed Augustine's theology as irrational (Freud thought that all religion was founded on neurosis), but he agreed with Augustine's observations on infantile vice. Unbroken by education, unfettered by their superego, babies—according to Freud—are bundles of scandalous urges. They worship their bellies; they hate work and love pleasure; they are angry and narcissistic; and they are—here is Freud's addition to the list of infantile vices—full of lust (especially toward their mothers) and murderous envy (especially toward their fathers).

Some of us have a more generous view of babies, but even the most optimistic have to concede that envy and jealousy (flipsides of the same coin) make their appearance very early in human development. Envy is the urge to have what the other possesses; jealousy is the bitter resentment you feel toward those who have what you want. Babies are jealous; young children are jealous; the old are jealous. This is human nature. Some people rarely feel anger; others are untouched by gluttony; lust often wanes as the years go by. But the green-eyed monster, with its malevolent gaze, pursues us from cradle to grave.[6]

Why is this so? Perhaps our selfish genes are at fault, as Richard Dawkins contends.[7] In times of scarcity, our genes seek to privilege our own lives at the expense of others' and to privilege the lives of our own children (who bear replicas of our genes) at the expense of the lives of other people's offspring. Whatever the explanation, humans tend to put themselves first. The Talmud grants full legitimacy to this instinct:

46

ENVY

"Two who were walking along a road, and in the hand of one of them is a flask of water; if both of them drink, they die, but if one drinks, he reaches a village. Ben Petora argued: 'It is better that they both drink and die—let not one of them see the death of his friend.' Until Rabbi Akiva came and taught: 'That your brother may live with you [Leviticus 25:36], your life takes precedence over the life of your brother.'"[8]

But what if we each have a flask? What if there is sufficient water (or milk, as Augustine observed) for everybody? Why do we still feel jealous, even though the well-being of others does not deprive us of anything? Perhaps because our unconscious is an ancient thinking-machine that obeys the logic of precapitalist economies. It cannot imagine a win-win situation in which everybody profits. Deep down, beneath the glossy surface of modern *Homo sapiens,* there lurks a more primitive Neanderthal who has never heard of Adam Smith or the principles of the free market. At our core, we live by a simple principle: wealth and pleasure are limited; what you get is taken from me; if you have it, I do not.[9] The Augustinian baby will not be generous unless all of its needs are fully and permanently satisfied.

It is hard to reach this blissful state of absolute satisfaction. Unfortunately, our parents do not live for us alone—they also live for themselves. Even when they hasten to carry out our wishes, they never do so fast enough. Our needs are never gratified instantly. That pause between desire and satisfaction is a source of frustration and anxiety. Worse still, others are even less eager than our parents to carry out our wishes. Our fathers and mothers have agendas which may even include the birth of brothers and sisters to compete with us, perhaps not for food but definitely for attention, for love, for toys.[10]

What makes all this difficult to bear is that there once *was* a time when we did not have to compete with anybody, when we felt protected and satisfied. The sons and daughters of Adam and Eve begin their lives, like their ancestors, in Paradise. They float, well sheltered, in warm amniotic fluid, linked to their mother through the umbilical cord. The needs of the fetus are satisfied without its having to make others aware of its distress—without having to cry, demand, or beg. The beating of its mother's heart resonates in its ears like a reassuring promise: "I am here; I am *always* here; I will never leave you for even a fraction of a second." The baby and its mother are one, in a world where only the two of them exist—a world where the baby possesses her completely. The existence of others is only a distant murmur without much significance.

This wonderful idyll is brutally interrupted at birth: the baby is expelled from its warm aquarium into a world of harsh colors, unfamiliar odors, and discordant sounds that confuse his senses. The umbilical cord is cut. No longer surrounded by the sound of the mother's beating heart, the newborn cries—stunned, betrayed, abandoned. The infant is forced to develop a consciousness. To be conscious entails pain. The Scriptures were wrong: we eat of the Tree of Knowledge only *after* the expulsion from Paradise. The infant learns to obtain by ruse or violence what it had once received without asking. The presence of others is threatening. How did they get there? Why do they stand in the way? The baby has no confidence in anybody. It wants to be reassured that the whole world is at its disposal, as was the case in the womb. The infant is angry at anyone who wants a share of the mother, such as its father, its siblings, the entire human race. It is jealous. I do not envy it.

Jealous people feel that something belonging to them by right, something they want (and desire makes right in the repressed parts of our consciousness: a thing is ours because we want it), is in the hands of someone else. Deep down, we feel that everything belongs to us—or at least should. In a better world, others would be able to enjoy only the toys we do not want. That others have things we want is a moral outrage. Growing up, the social animal is taught to be ashamed of this feeling and is forced to accept that the world does not belong to it alone. Others also have rights, which we must respect. We are expected to share and be good sports, to accept gallantly the successes of others. We

ENV Y

are expected to smile as others get a larger share, a prettier woman, a more handsome man, a more enthusiastic round of applause. Of course, we have to accept reality—but don't expect us to enjoy it. Listen carefully and you'll hear the quiet sound of gnashing teeth.

In all societies, great effort is expended on uprooting envy by means of education; we are taught to share, to repress our envy. Failure to repress such feelings is a sign of weakness. We would all prefer to be without envy. But how? Wouldn't it be wonderful if we simply possessed everything and had no need to feel envy? Unfortunately, this is impossible; it was impossible even in the Garden of Eden. All that Adam and Eve lacked were the forbidden fruits of the Tree of Knowledge and the Tree of Life. Why were our ancestors eager to get these fruits? Was it really the need to know good and evil, or even to live forever? This is hard to believe. The former would have added nothing to their happiness—quite the contrary: "In much wisdom there is much grief, and he who increases knowledge increases sorrow."[11] As for the latter, would someone who has just been born, who has his whole life ahead of him, really take risks in order to gain immortality? Young people are not afraid of death. The quest for immortality is a preoccupation of the old.

It was envy that spurred Adam and Eve to eat the fruit of the Tree of Knowledge. There existed a being greater than themselves—a being who had made the rules and could change them at will, who had planted the trees and could eat any fruit He wanted, because everything, everything, belonged to Him. It was this that Adam and Eve could not bear. They ate the fruit of knowledge not in order to know good and evil, but in order to be like God.

Humans covet what they do not have, but God has everything. It is therefore surprising that envy is one of His signal characteristics in the Bible. In Hebrew, there is no distinction between envy and jealousy. A single word, *qin'ah,* is used for both. In chapter 34 of Exodus, God declares that His name is Qan'a, or "Jealous." God wants everything that other gods have, and He resents His own people's dealings with them. "Break down their altars, smash their sacred stones, and cut down their Asherah poles. Do not worship any other god, for the Lord whose name is Jealous is a jealous God."[12] If Jealous were a man, we would say that he suffers from serious insecurity and from dangerous outbursts of jealous violence. But since He is God, and a jealous god, it is better to glorify Him and to marvel at the impenetrable nature of His ways.

When Jealous feels threatened, He breaks and destroys other children's toys. Sometimes He breaks and destroys the children. After the episode of the Golden Calf, for example, Jealous is not content with burning the calf and reducing it to ashes. His anger subsides only after the members of the tribe of Levi have killed, on His orders, three thousand Children of Israel. This behavioral pattern is repeated on other occasions. Jealous punishes His people for any association with other gods. Jews, Christians, and Muslims are so accustomed to this type of divine behavior (Allah conducts himself in a similar way) that we are rarely astonished by it. But why would it be justifiable to punish with such savagery the petty infidelities of the faithful? After all, aren't they just virtual infidelities? Aren't other gods merely illusions, fantastic beings lacking all substance? What excites the anger of Jealous is not so much the consequences of the Israelites' infidelities, but their motivation. He cannot bear the idea that He is not their sole object of desire, that they are *capable* of desiring another.

All this brings to mind the behavior of jealous husbands: incessant suspicion, threats, spying on their wives, violent outbursts in reaction to real or imagined infidelities. The Bible often uses the metaphor of adultery to describe the propensity of the Israelites to "have dealings with" other gods. They play the role of the adulterous woman, and God plays that of the jealous, cuckolded husband. The prophet Ezekiel is particularly fond of this metaphor. In chapter 16, he rails against the betrayal of the Israelites in crude sexual terms: "At the head of every street you built your lofty shrines and degraded your beauty, offering your body with increasing promiscuity to anyone who passed by. You engaged in prostitution with the Egyptians, your lustful neighbors, and provoked me to anger with your increasing promiscuity."[13] And in chapter 23: "Then the Babylonians came to her, to the bed of love, and in their lust they defiled her. After she had been defiled by them, she turned away from them in disgust. When she carried on her prostitution openly and exposed her nakedness, I turned away from her in disgust, just as I had turned away from her sister. Yes, she became more and more promiscuous as she recalled the days of her youth, when she was a prostitute in Egypt. There she lusted after her lovers, whose genitals were like those of donkeys and whose emission was like that of horses. So you longed for the lewdness of your youth, when in Egypt your bosom was caressed and your young breasts fondled."[14] It is not only the choice of another (or of others) that makes the divine blood boil, but also the implied sexual prowess of the lusty neighbors to whom the unfaithful wife is attracted. They have genitals "like those of donkeys" and emission "like that of horses." This is why she is attracted to them, the whore.

As a cuckold, God is no different from mortal males. The cuckold is the object of endless scorn, the ridiculous butt of a thousand comedies. His wife's infidelity is a symbolic castration. She is seeking her pleasures elsewhere because he is not man enough. It is to avoid such a fate worse than death that most human cultures legitimate, legally and morally, the right of a man to be jealous over his woman. The Bible sanctions this right, and God Himself serves as a collaborator of the jealous husband:

> If any man's wife goes astray and behaves unfaithfully toward him, and a man lies with her carnally, and it is hidden

51

from the eyes of her husband, and it is concealed that she has defiled herself, and there was no witness against her, nor was she caught—if the spirit of jealousy comes upon him and he becomes jealous of his wife, who has defiled herself; or if the spirit of jealousy comes upon him and he becomes jealous of his wife, although she has not defiled herself—then the man shall bring his wife to the priest. He shall bring the offering required for her, one-tenth of an ephah of barley meal; he shall pour no oil on it and put no frankincense on it, because it is a grain offering of jealousy, an offering for remembering, for bringing iniquity to remembrance.[15]

The priest makes the suspect wife drink "bitter water that brings the curse." If she is indeed guilty of adultery, her unfaithfulness is revealed by God by means of the ordeal, and she is stoned to death. This is a highly unusual procedure in Hebrew law. Hebrew law is firmly opposed to ordeals. Furthermore, the procedure allows an accuser to impose a judicial process on the accused with no evidence whatsoever that an offense has been committed—not even hearsay. The only justification for this elaborate and dangerous ritual is the purely subjective anxiety of the husband. In all other cases, suspicion is not enough; but being cuckolded has such disastrous consequences that exceptions to the rules are deemed necessary.

All means are justified to avoid cuckoldry. Upon this article of faith, cultures have erected superb edifices—poems, novels, epic tales—praising faithful women to the skies and vilifying the less faithful as whores. The man who covets his neighbor's goods is worthy of social scorn; the man who fails to hide his bitterness at his friend's success is treated with disdain. The jealousy of a man over his wife, in contrast, is sanctioned and glorified by all patriarchal cultures. Very often, the woman suspected of adultery does not even make it to court. The man whose honor had been assailed, and members of his offended family, can exact their own justice, with the explicit or implicit permission of the legal system. Jealousy gives men a license to kill. In the sacred name of honor, a jealous man can inspire terror in the hearts of women under his authority and force them into submission that extends far beyond the realms of sexual purity. Since the entire body of the woman is defined as a ticking sex bomb ("a woman's hair is sexual"; "a woman's voice is sexual"—everything about a woman is sexual),[16] men demanded complete authority to shackle it, to limit its movements, to hide it, to prevent numerous activities that would have allowed the owner of that body to participate in the activities of the public sphere. The woman is part of the household. She belongs in the house.[17]

And what about women? Don't they feel jealousy? Of course they do. Jealousy is an integral part of human nature. But poets have rarely praised and celebrated women's jealousy, and legislators have never given the jealous woman a license to kill. A devoted woman is permitted to be jealous as an expression of love, for it is often assumed (wrongly, in my opinion) that true love desires exclusivity. But whereas a man's obsessive jealousy is treated with sympathy (in fact, most cultures would go a long way before declaring a man's jealousy "obsessive"), a woman who tries to impose her jealousy on her man is "hysterical." Jealous women make mountains out of molehills. They fail to take into account the natural needs and urges of the male of the species. Men have little sympathy for them.

But one is allowed to feel sympathy for the victims of excessive male jealousy—if they are totally innocent, that is. We feel sympathy for the many Desdemonas smothered by their Othellos, "who loved not wisely but too well."[18] The real villain is Iago, who is not protecting his own property or sexual honor, but avenging a slight to his ego: he covets his friend's success and well-deserved status. Iago is despicable,

Othello tragic. The implication is that Othello's lethal instincts, though misdirected, were neither minor nor undignified. What if Desdemona did have an affair with Cassio? Why, in a culture that places a much greater value on the soul than on the body, is having sexual relations with Cassio so much more offensive than having a meaningful platonic relationship with him? We rarely get satisfying answers to these questions. We're simply told that that's the way things are. In the past (and, if Hollywood is an indication, in the present too) it would be practically impossible for an adulterous woman to win our sympathy—except, that is, if we consider the husband she cuckolds to be unworthy of respect. Only when the husband is either an enemy whose humiliation we crave, or a "natural" cuckold (an unmanly man whose sexual possessions are free game), do we side, half-heartedly, with the unfaithful woman. Needless to say, society's sympathy for unfaithful men is a great deal stronger.

In general, our empathy for female victims is reserved for the immaculately faithful. Women of ancient times understood this only too well—and if they did not, the edifying stories that males wrote for them helped to drive the message home. Consider the story of Lucretia, wife of Lucius Collatinus, that was told to generations of little girls and boys in the Roman world. When the unhappy Lucretia is raped by Sextus Tarquinius, son of the wicked king Lucius Tarquinius Superbus, she realizes it will be difficult for her to exonerate herself. How can her husband know that she didn't provoke the rape by being "slutty"? When her husband returns, she swears before the gods that she is innocent, but she also knows that doubt will always remain in the jealous man's heart. Besides, she is now damaged goods. Better to wipe the slate clean. "What can be well with a woman who has lost her honor? In your bed, Collatinus, are the marks of another man," she declares to her husband. "My body only has been violated. My heart is innocent, and death will be my witness."[19] Only death can redeem Lucretia, transforming her from a dubious woman into a heroine worthy of admiration in the eyes of young Roman girls. A woman who was raped in her home and who did not wash her tarnished body with her own blood would always remain an embarrassment to her husband.[20]

In the past century, masculine jealousy has lost some of its force and glory in the West. The West, we are told, has "liberated" its women. "Defending" the (male) family honor no longer occupies the central cultural role it once had. The woman's body has gone through a process of de-eroticization in the public sphere. Parts of the female body that, in the not-so-distant past, were deemed capable of driving a man mad with desire or jealousy have been redefined as harmless and fit for decent exposure. Whereas in patriarchal societies a woman's hair, ankle, thigh, cleavage, shoulder, and even the nape of her neck were thought to provoke sexual frenzy, now only the region of the sexual organs is considered off-limits for public display. All the rest can be bared with impunity. This shows the extent to which sexuality and sexual jealousy are conditioned by culture, and how much the "irrepressible instinct" of man is only a myth.[21] Western males have flexible sexual triggers that allow them to react according to the context. Buttocks and breasts—even total nudity—are considered legitimate on a European beach. Women who undress there are not considered promiscuous. A respectable woman can thus show herself in public almost naked, as men have always done.

All this does not mean that men have lost their capacity to be stimulated by the sight of the female body. It means that they have more control over their impulses than they care to admit. Modern men have learned to contain their impulses, as women have always been constrained to do. It is an interesting process. Consider the medieval doctor: upper-class women would not expose their bodies in front of a stranger, except perhaps to bare their wrists so a physician could take their pulse. Any contact by a man, whoever he was, with the covered parts of the female body was perceived as a sexual act. In the sixteenth century, surgeons began—in France and then elsewhere—to develop a new theory allowing them to rid the profession of their competitors, the midwives, who until then had played an important role as "touchers" of women.[22] Midwives could dispense gynecological treatment without harming the reputation of a female patient and without arousing the suspicion of the father or the jealousy of the husband. Though surgeons could not change their sex when attending female patients, they began to claim that their sexual drives were neutralized while they were acting as professionals. They could see nude patients, palpate women's breasts, and introduce their fingers into vaginas without arousing their own (and presumably the women's) sexual desires.

Nobody has ever tried to prove this claim scientifically. Does the doctor become a eunuch when treating a female patient? And what about the female patient—has she lost her sexual appetite simply because the man penetrating her declares himself sexually indifferent? This is hard to believe. It is more plausible that, from time to time, doctors do feel sexual arousal at some level and that at least some female patients, from time to time, are stimulated sexually by contact with the doctor. Yet what matters is not whether doctors have erections, or whether women are sexually aroused by their physicians' probings, but how flexible, how artificial, the boundaries of sexual propriety—and consequently the boundaries of legitimate sexual jealousy—can be.

The myth of the desexualized therapeutic situation was rapidly accepted and took on the force of dogma. Men no longer felt threatened by the fact that their wives were isolated in a room with a man who was touching their bodies, and doctors did not rape women en masse. In general, they managed to behave "professionally," with the required detachment. It is thus evident that men are able to neutralize their sexual urges, at least sufficiently to control their behavior. If they have a good reason to control themselves, males can, and do, maintain control. It is a matter of choice, for these same men are capable of being excited at the sight of the female body as soon as they take off their white coats. Is the plug connected or disconnected? The differences in behavior are spectacular. The decision to be "on" or "off" depends to a large extent on ourselves and on the margin of maneuver that our culture allows us.

In the West, then, jealousy, like adultery, has largely passed from the public sphere to the private and from the courtroom to the therapist's office. But privatization did not rid us of jealousy's heartaches. *Invidia* is not a fun vice. Its victims, both male and female, suffer when their partners manifest interest in someone else. One easily recognizes the symptoms of the partner's interest suddenly switching on: the excitement, the sudden erotic tension in the air, the unconscious sexual clues (wandering hands, furtive touches, lingering looks, slightly too much closeness between your partner and the other).[23] As the Israeli singer-songwriter Meir Ariel says in his "Song of Pain": "She would go to her meeting once a week / and always come back with a flushed cheek / with a certain heavy breathing I haven't seen in years. / Her 'I'm alive' look would stab me into tears." Worse than knowing that your mate is interested in another is the moment when these telltale signs go underground, when you realize that she's now trying to hide from you what had begun unconsciously, almost as a reflex. And worse still is the sudden flare of the jealous imagination: the vague and not-so-vague images of an intimacy both familiar and strange; the fear of losing your partner, your dignity, your mind. You repeat mentally the adult mantras: such things happen; it's no big deal; this has happened to me, too; it isn't that serious. You act like an adult, but something in this situation throws us back to an infantile state, igniting the burning embers of insecurity and the anger that often accompanies it. There's a classic Israeli children's song that always brings tears to my eyes:

Mom said to Danny: "My boy is clever and cool;
My boy will never cry his eyes out, like a silly little fool."

"I never cry, Mommy; I'm not a baby; I am grown.
But why, Mommy, please tell me, do the tears cry on their
     own?

I gave Nurit a flower, I gave her an apple bright red;
I gave Nurit a toy, gave her everything I had.
Nurit ate my apple; she threw the flower away;
She then saw another boy and went out with him to play.

I never cry mommy; I'm not a baby; I am grown.
But why, Mommy, please tell me, do the tears cry on their
     own?"[24]

It is easy to pass from jealousy to self-pity.

Enough of sexual jealousy. Sexual jealousy in the West is like that out-dated jacket we hide in the back of our closet. It's still there, but we're ashamed to wear it in public. In contrast, there's another aspect of envy that has *not* gone out of fashion in the West—namely, covetousness. "You shall not covet your neighbor's wife, or his manservant or maidservant, his ox or donkey, or anything that belongs to your neighbor."[25] In the West, covetousness has ceased to be considered a vice and has become a great virtue. It is perhaps wrong to covet the ass and cow of your neighbor, but it is highly recommended to want an ass and a cow of the very same model.

Jealousy and covetousness have a common foundation—the implicit assumption that possession is the key to happiness—but the jealous husband and the covetous neighbor are looking at it from vastly different vantage points. If you have something I want, I'm all for sharing; if you want something I have, I become a firm believer in the sacred right of ownership. The covetous society is an attempt to reconcile the two: you can't have what's mine, but you can have something just like it.

It is possible, as I said earlier, that our unconscious remains the prisoner of a precapitalist conception of the world; but society has certainly evolved. One of the fundamental principles of nonindustrial societies is contentment. "Who is a rich man? A man who is content with his lot."[26] One must be content with one's lot and not question the principles of social allocation. If you are poor, be happy with what you have. If you are a slave, if you are exploited or cheated, do not complain. At most, you can hope for a different lot in the world to come. In the Kingdom of Heaven, wealth is unlimited. There, the righteous will enjoy perpetual abundance. In earthly kingdoms, unfortunately, things are different. Here, a man must know his place.

Jesus himself, herald of a revolutionary religious outlook, remained conservative on the social level. Blessed are the poor, for theirs is the Kingdom of Heaven. Blessed are the persecuted. Jesus was concerned not with making this world a better place, but with ushering in the Kingdom. There, nothing needs fixing; here, nothing can be fixed. While they await the coming of the Kingdom, the faithful should rejoice in what they have. This world, after all, is nothing but a brief interval on the route to our heavenly home, where the last shall be first. Saint Paul says it very clearly:

> Each one should retain the place in life that the Lord assigned to him and to which God has called him. . . . Each one should remain in the situation which he was in when God called him. Were you a slave when you were called? Don't let it trouble you—although if you can gain your freedom, do so. For he who was a slave when he was called by the Lord is the Lord's freedman; similarly, he who was a free man when he was called is Christ's slave. You were

bought at a price; do not become slaves of men. Brothers, each man, as responsible to God, should remain in the situation God called him to.[27]

All this is quite irresponsible economically. Ask Milton Friedman. If everybody were content with what he or she has, there would be no economic growth; without economic growth, progress would cease and we would fall back into the "Dark Ages" (and lose a lot of money).

We don't like losing money. In a process that began in the twelfth century and triumphed decisively with the Industrial Revolution in the 1800s, Western society rejected the principle of sobriety and of contentment with one's lot, in favor of a holy unending thirst for more—more money, more cars, more possessions, more of the more. Buy and you shall be blessed. Blessed are the rich, for theirs is the Kingdom of Earth (forget the Kingdom of Heaven—it's a terrible investment; leave it to the poor).

Consumer society is based on encouraging covetousness. You want your neighbors' toys. Advertising flaunts their wealth and their commercially produced happiness like a red flag before your eyes. They are happy because they consume, because they possess. How can you be inferior to them? Why don't you possess those clothes, that house, that car, those vacations, that woman, that man? You should work more and buy more, for you are never content with what you have. If you have less than your neighbor (and you always have less), you are jealous. This is good.

It's easy to perceive only the unpleasant—greedy, materialistic, obsessive—aspects of this worldview; but one must remember that it is also the basis of the Western impulse to cast off patriarchy and despotism, and that it expresses, despite its faults and its hypocrisy, the egalitarian ideals of society. The citizen of the consumer society is green with envy. He surreptitiously eyes his neighbor's grass. He is not satisfied with what he has, because he thinks he ought to have more; he

ENVY

thinks his lawn should be greener. Since Western society does not allow him to set fire to his neighbor's lawn or take possession of it by force, he has no choice but try to grow a lawn just as green. There is something disagreeable about this restlessness. It smacks of sweat and pettiness. How undignified the Western materialist appears, compared with the serene and otherworldly Buddhist monk or Muslim Sufi mystic![28] Yet it is no accident that the monk and the Sufi, happy though they may be with what they have, find themselves living in a world of shocking inequalities and injustices. In the West, those who covet have produced an ideology of equality—if not of goods, then at least (if only in principle, and only in some parts of this world) of opportunity.

The problem with equal opportunity is that often it is only a fiction. If you work hard and make an effort, then you too will possess that Ferrari and that corporate jet. If you do not succeed, that's your problem. You had equal opportunity, didn't you? Well, not quite. We shall return to these questions in the chapter devoted to greed. To understand people's behavior, we have to ask ourselves, like the Roman consul Cassius, "Cui bono?"—"Whom does it profit?" Envy, instilled in us by millions of commercials promoting obsessive consumption, profits a handful of very rich people. And what about the rest of us? It's perhaps time for us to reconsider the old computer, the old washing machine, the old television. Perhaps these are sufficient for our needs. Perhaps the grass in our backyard is green enough.

LUST
Luxuria

Why do the daughters of the uncircumcised rejoice?[1] Here is one explanation:

> For when an uncircumcised man wishes to sleep with a beautiful woman, she will use sweet words to lure him to her, and his mind shall become obsessed with being with her every day. And he shall exhaust himself with craving intercourse. And that woman shall ensnare a man uncircumcised in the flesh and lie in his bosom in her passion, for indeed he thrusts inside her a long time because of the foreskin, which is a barrier against ejaculation in intercourse. Thus, she feels pleasure and emits seed [reaches an orgasm] first. When the uncircumcised man sleeps with her and then resolves to return to his home, she brazenly grasps him, holding on to his genitals, and says to him, "Come back, copulate." This is because of the pleasure that she finds in intercourse with him, from his awe-inspiring penis, an iron penis—and from his equine ejaculation,[2] which he shoots like an arrow into her womb. They are united without separating, and he has her twice and three

times in one night, and [their] appetite is not filled. And so he does with her night after night. The sexual activity emaciates him of his bodily fat and afflicts his flesh, and he corrupts his brain entirely in women's affairs, an evil corruption, and his mind is thus demolished. Between her legs he sank, he fell.[3] And he cannot see the light of the King's presence, for the eyes of his mind have been shut, and he can no longer see the light.

But when a circumcised man desires the beauty of women, and cleaves to his wife, or to another woman comely in appearance, he finds himself performing his task quickly, emitting his seed as soon as he inserts the crown. And when he has slept with her once, he rests, satisfied, and will not know her again for seven more days. And this is the circumcised man's custom with the woman he loves: he has an orgasm first and cannot restrain himself. As soon as he begins intercourse with her, he immediately ejaculates and she has no pleasure from him when she lies down or when she arises. And it would be better for her if he had not known her and had not come near her at all, for he arouses her heat to no avail and she remains in a state of desire for a man even as the semen is still in her "reservoir," frustrated and confounded. She does not emit seed even once a year except on rare occasions, when because of the great heat and the fire burning within her, she emits seed first. But he [the circumcised man] says, "I am the Lord's." For he would not empty his brain because of the woman that lies in his bosom or the wife of his friend. He will find grace, and his mind good favor; his heart will be strong to seek out God, and he shall not fear gazing at Him. And if He speaks to him, he shall not turn his back.

Thus, the woman has more pleasure with the uncircumcised than with the circumcised, and she kills him with her desire and crushes his brain with it.[4] And it is not out of malice or by his own hand; he is a man killed by women. As we are taught in *Berechit Rabba:* "A woman who has sexual relations with an uncircumcised man will find it hard to separate from him." We have explained above that this text deals with the case of Dinah [daughter of Jacob, raped by Shechem the Hivite] or another beautiful Israelite woman who enjoyed copulating with an uncircumcised (Jew or non-Jew) more than with a circumcised man. For wise Nature has ordered that the male and female enjoy each other's embraces. But even the best of the uncircumcised, a man with a pure heart, fearing God and fleeing sin, is attacked by desire every day and he fights against it every night, because of the foreskin that gives him no respite, and he occupies himself all the days of his life with escaping the traps it holds for him. This is why his mind is not ready to be presented before the King, because of his enemies at the gate. And God will not appear to the uncircumcised, for he fears approaching Him, because of the enemy raging in his home. But He will show himself to the circumcised man, who stands in the Temple calm and sure of himself, for no enemy awaits him. He can purify his mind when he wants and contemplate the image of God.[5]

These words from the thirteenth-century commentary on *Bamidbar Rabba* by Rabbi Isaac ben Yedaa'iah are a good way to begin an examination of lust. It is a powerful text—totally far-fetched in its discussion of circumcised men, of course. Certain explicit and implicit assumptions in this somewhat embarrassingly autobiographical text by the Provençal sage are worth noting. First, Rabbi Isaac believes (like Maimonides)[6] that circumcision weakens virility and diminishes sexual pleasure. Second, he thinks that the uncircumcised man, despite his impressive virility and staying power—with his awe-inspiring (literally "frightening") penis of iron and the horse-like sperm he ejaculates like an arrow—remains a pitiful victim, the victim of women, both Jewish and non-Jewish. Members of the "weaker sex" are described as lascivious creatures, carried away by insatiable desire. They rape the unfortunate uncircumcised man. His wicked foreskin prevents him from effectively defending himself and brings about his downfall. His member thrusts and thrusts, the women have orgasms, and all the while his flesh is wasting away and his brain is withering, until he falls between the woman's legs like Sisera between the legs of Jaël.[7] His body is broken and his brain shattered. Third, perhaps to our surprise, Rabbi Isaac isn't in the least apologetic about the wretched performance of the Jewish man. This serial frustrater of women who "performs his task quickly" and infrequently, whose wife has an orgasm only once a year (no thanks to him), turns out to be stronger than the uncircumcised macho male. For the very same physical inferiority that makes him pathetic in our eyes wins him grace in the eyes of God. The Jewish man is potent where it really counts: in spirit.

For Rabbi Isaac, Jewish circumcision is not unlike female "circumcision" (the removal of parts of the female genitalia, especially the clitoris) in that it transforms sexual relations from a ruinous feast of desire and pleasure into an act which affords little pleasure. Mutilated men and women "perform" for the sole purpose of procreation or at the most the fulfillment of a (religious) duty—to prevent their partner from seeking dangerous liaisons outside the home. This destruction of pleasure is cruel—the rabbi is not without sympathy for the poor wife of the circumcised man. Night after night she experiences nothing but frustration. Even her annual orgasm has little joy in it. But lovemaking is not about love. It is a game in which all the participants are victims. Even the energy-sucking vamp who brazenly grabs the uncircumcised man's genitals and forces him to pleasure her is not a dominatrix but a slave, a plaything in the hands of the implacable boy-god Eros. A Jew is not allowed to choose celibacy. Whether he likes it or not, he's in the game. Circumcision deprives Eros of his trump card. Having quickly sated his sexual drive, the Jewish man can, in Rabbi Isaac's words, "stand in the Temple calm and sure of himself."

If only it were so easy. Sex is dangerous. It is dangerous because it promises intense and straightforward pleasure, pleasure that every person can understand. Unlike the Kingdom of Heaven, a real orgasm is self-explanatory. If you're *not* sure, you probably haven't had one. This unmediated gratification threatens the established order, because it is totally amoral. A person is not necessarily attracted to the right partners, or to the right acts. Indeed, stolen water tastes sweeter than holy water.[8] Man is a battlefield: "I see another law at work in the members of my body," declares Saint Paul, "waging war against the law of my mind and making me a prisoner of the law of sin at work within my members."[9] The rabbis, somewhat less dramatically, concur. "When a man's passions are stirred and he is about to commit an act of debauchery, all his limbs are ready to obey him, . . . but when he is about to perform an act of piety, all his limbs become sluggish, because the evil inclination [*yetser ha-ra*] in his entrails holds sway over the two hundred forty-eight limbs of his body, whereas the good inclination [*yetser ha-tov*] is like one who is confined in prison."[10] The power of Eros to corrupt us, to drag us kicking and screaming into debauchery, is a scandal. But the outrage doesn't end with arousal; it gets worse. Instead of being attracted to the modest and bashful daughters of Israel, men lust after the lecherous daughters of the uncircumcised—just as, far from being attracted to the sensitive new man, liberated women secretly lust after the testosterone-dripping macho type. It isn't us. Lust made us do it.

It is thus not surprising that the mystics chose erotic metaphors to describe their love for God.[11] They were looking for images powerful enough to express that love. The calm intellectual observation of Rabbi

Isaac's circumcised man? Surely that does not do justice to the mystic's love for God. The sexual frenzy of the uncircumcised man and his voracious women, the force that possesses us, drives us mad, makes us lose our heads and forget the knowledge of good and evil—this is the only way the mystic can adequately describe his passion for God. Only erotic love and death (Eros and Thanatos) can provide analogies strong enough to convey the impossible and the scandalous—the union of human and divine.

In his revolutionary sermons on the Song of Songs—the sole book of the Bible that celebrates erotic love—Saint Bernard, abbot of Clairvaux, mixes metaphors brilliantly. The Word is made Flesh; flesh is made words; and the two meet in the kiss of "His" mouth. "Of what use to me the wordy effusions of the Prophets? Rather, let Him who is 'the most handsome of the sons of men'—let Him kiss me with a kiss of His mouth. No longer am I satisfied to listen to Moses, for he is a slow speaker and not able to speak well.' Isaiah is 'a man of unclean lips.' Jeremiah does not know how to speak; he is a child. Not one of the prophets makes an impact on me with his words. But He, the one whom they proclaim—let Him speak to me, 'let Him kiss me with the kiss of His mouth.'"[12] It is permissible to desire God, to lust after Him, to crave His kisses and what comes after the kisses. But this fleshing out of spiritual love for God does not legitimize carnal love in the eyes of the pious. It comes in its stead. "Love," notes Rabbi Shimon Bar Yochai—allegedly the author of the Zohar—"corrupts the laws."[13] Lust corrupts entire legal codes. It is better to corset it with prohibitions and interdictions, with taboos and regulations, especially when women—those strange creatures who have the power to turn the world upside down—are involved.

In the later Middle Ages, a story that enjoyed enormous popularity related how Aristotle, the greatest of the Greek philosophers, and his capitulation to lust. Aristotle, we are told, had rebuked his student Alexander the Great for being too attached to his young mistress, Phyllis. This attachment was spiritually dangerous. The philosopher advised the future conqueror of Asia to leave her. Grudgingly but obligingly, Alexander decided to consent, and word of this reached Phyllis. One morning, she went to the garden in front of the philosopher's window. She sang in her lovely voice and walked about in the garden, flaunting the charms of her magnificent body. Aristotle, seized with lust, begged her to grant him her favors. She agreed. There was one condition: the philosopher had to go down on all fours and let her ride on his back. A man seized by lust will do almost anything. While Aristotle gamboled like a horse in the garden with Phyllis on his back, Alexander watched through the window, and the image he saw was more powerful than a thousand words. This would not have surprised Rabbi Isaac. Like the poor uncircumcised gentile, Aristotle was just another man killed by women.[14]

Sexual attraction must be regulated, if we do not want men of good repute to make fools of themselves and women of ill repute to gain the upper hand. All societies, even the most permissive, impose limits on the sexual choices of their members. The taboo against sexual relations between mother and son (though not necessarily other incestuous relations) seems universal, and most societies have a great many additional prohibitions. Usually there are many more prohibitions than this taboo. The sexual act is perceived as a physical and metaphysical union, blurring the boundaries of the self and capable of generating strange and dangerous mixtures. When this union involves beings of different species, it engenders "monsters." The world abounds with stories describing half-human, half-bestial creatures born from forbidden relations between men (or gods) and animals.[15] Even Yahweh was not immune to the dangers of hybridity: "When men began to increase in number on the earth and daughters were born to them, the sons of God saw that the daughters of men were beautiful, and they took any of them they chose. Then Yahweh said: 'My Spirit will not contend with man forever, for he is mortal.' . . . The Nephilim were on the earth in those days—and also afterward—when the sons of God went to the daughters of men and had children by them."[16] Ah, those beautiful daughters of men! Three verses later, Yahweh decides to wipe mankind off the face of the earth. He could try forbidding His sons to fraternize, but how likely were they to listen? The problem with the mixing brought about by sex is that its damage is not only physical but moral. It is the closest thing Judaism has to a concept of original sin passed on from generation to generation: "No bastard nor any of his descendants, even down to the tenth generation, may enter the assembly of Yahweh."[17]

Forbidden unions are defined as types of "impurity"—the term that society applies to what it considers abominable and dangerous.[18] Proscribed are—among other things—intercourse with blood relations (incest), copulation with children (child abuse), same-sex relations (homosexuality or, to use the more traditional word, sodomy), relations with animals (bestiality), and masturbation (self-abuse). Definitions vary, of course, depending on which relations count as incest, who is considered a child, what constitutes homosexuality, and so forth. But all sexual prohibitions are born of moral outrage. Trespasses are not technical irregularities, like tax evasion; they are abominations that render offenders despicable and contagious—like infectious disease.[19]

Sexual prohibitions concern the infringement not only of biological distinctions (those between men, women, children, animals) but also of social divides. Patriarchal societies forbid sexual relations that transgress social boundaries (between free man and slave, between clan member and foreigner, between high and low castes).[20] These bans seek to limit the sexual freedom of social inferiors, especially women. Women have no honor of their own to maintain, at least in the public sphere ("The honor of the king's daughter is entirely within [the palace]"),[21] but they can, and often do, dishonor their men. They do so when they have any sexual relationship that is not sanctioned by those who hold authority over them. Women undermine the established order, even when they are overly interested in *"legitimate"* sex. The ideal woman is modest and pious. Whatever traces of lust she has in her are directed exclusively to her husband. The Jewish woman has a right to a certain number of conjugal relations, referred to as her *onah*—her "season."[22] But as we have seen with Rabbi Isaac ben Yedaa'iah, this is a matter of quantity, not quality. The wife is entitled to conjugal relations once a week, as is demanded of *talmidei hachamim* (those who study the Torah), but "she does not emit seed even once a year."

If a woman went beyond the walls built by society, she was risking her life. Insubordinate women threaten the very foundations of the home. They must be removed from decent company, or, if that isn't enough, from the realm of the living. Yet despite all the threats, despite the extensive legal, cultural, and pedagogical system devised to make inferiors toe the line, lines are crossed. There will always be individuals who trespass, as an act of protest or, more frequently, of passion. But whatever the reasons, in patriarchal societies (and in many "post-patriarchal" ones as well) sexual offenses are seen not as private choices, but as public rebellion against sacred social values. Sex is political and hierarchical. There is a right way of doing it: superiors demonstrate control over inferiors by penetrating them. Copulation expresses possession and domination (in Hebrew, "to copulate" is *lib'ol*, meaning "to possess," and the husband is *ba'al*, "the one who possesses"). Inferiors are forbidden to "possess" what by right belongs to their superiors.

In past centuries, men of high social status often had the right to "possess" those in their power. It went without saying that women captured in war (divided as booty among the victors) were free game for their new masters, whatever the women's religious, social, and marital status. Consent was not required. A free Roman male was allowed a wide range of "penetration" space to express his status and satisfy his sexual needs. He could copulate at will with his slaves—male and female, adults and minors. Semi-ritualized rape was often performed as an act of "breaking" subordinates. But this went only in one direction: a master who allowed himself to be "penetrated" by his slave was condemned to death for social high treason.[23] Even today, in societies where intercourse between males is not outlawed, social aggressiveness (contempt, derision, physical violence) toward passive homosexuals is far worse than toward active homosexuals. A male "possessed" is an outrage to his sex.

The symbolic and physical violence unleashed in reaction to forbidden passions and the shocking cruelty with which offenders are punished express recognition of the fact that social boundaries are not *really* impenetrable. Lust shows that the social hierarchy is artificial. Illegitimate and mixed-race children are embarrassing evidence that the powerful and the weak are truly of the same species.[24] Violence is an implicit admission of failure—for the more severe the penalties, the more devastating each infringement of the rules. The obligation to use violence proves that the system has not succeeded in teaching the weak to internalize the rules of the powerful. A well-trained dog never needs the leash. A dog that must be beaten repeatedly gnaws at its master's authority. Human beings are not dogs. No matter how well one trains them, they always want to pursue happiness in their own way.

But one never stops trying. Patriarchal societies are heavily invested in their social hierarchies and are disinclined to see sex as a free-for-all game. Men are not born equal, and women certainly are not equal to men. Society's male authority figures are determined to tame desire. This is not easy. It takes both positive and negative measures. In monotheistic religions, the sexual act is described not as physical pleasure for the sake of pleasure, but as a sacred ritual governed by complex rules of the licit and illicit. Only the morally depraved copulate with no added spiritual element (love, procreation, the urge to do God's will). Even between partners whose union is authorized or perhaps blessed by society, there are right and wrong ways of performing the sexual act. There are preliminary rituals, and purity laws (principally linked to female secretions). Pleasure, even when it is not categorically denounced (as among certain extreme Christian ascetics), is a bonus, not the main objective of the act.

All religions require a measure of restraint from their adherents.[25] Marriage ceremonies signify a community's right to exercise control over human pleasure. Yet one is not only obliged to avoid forbidden liaisons; one must respect certain rules even during intercourse with a licit partner (purity rules, for example). Christian theologians, in line with Saint Paul's teaching, regarded sex with suspicion and believed that orgasm—the instant of uncontrolled pleasure, without which no conception is possible—was a vestige of original sin. This linking of pleasure and procreation obviously applies to males, but in the Middle Ages it was commonly applied to women as well. The Roman physician Galen, whose authority in medical matters rivaled that of Aristotle, taught that women, too, emit seed at the moment of orgasm (a view shared by Rabbi Isaac, as we have seen). But even theologians who did not accept the two-seed theory (rejected by Aristotle) rarely paused to wonder about the theological implications of women's conceiving without orgasm. Theirs was a world seen from the male perspective (in which women were considered half-baked men whose sexual organs were male organs turned inside out). For them, orgasm was the instant when the primordial blemish passed from generation to generation.[26]

Prior to original sin, humans could increase and multiply in the most civilized way, without emotional sound and fury or loss of control.[27] The male member, like other parts of Adam's body, was entirely under the control of the father of mankind. At will, Adam's member became hard; at will, it softened again. After the catastrophe of original sin, this power was lost. Sometimes a man wants his member to harden and it remains soft. Sometimes he wants it to remain soft and it stubbornly hardens. It seems to have a mind of its own. Women are even worse: in ancient times, their entire psyche was seen as being dominated by their sexual needs and by their uterus (Greek *hystera*), which was perceived as a living creature roving within the female body, demanding to be fed (by intercourse) and causing hysteria. In the *Timaeus*, Plato (who, as we shall see, viewed both male and female desire with suspicion) writes:

> This is why, of course, the male genitals are unruly and self-willed, like an animal that will not be subject to reason and, driven crazy by its desires, seeks to overpower everything else. The very same causes operate in women. A woman's womb or uterus, as it is called, is a living thing within her that desires childbearing. Now, when this creature remains unfruitful for an unseasonably long period of time, it becomes extremely frustrated and travels everywhere up and down her body. It blocks up her respiratory passages, and, by not allowing her to breathe, it throws her into extreme emergencies, and visits all sorts of other illnesses upon her.[28]

For the Church Fathers, humans' loss of control over their own bodies was not part of the nature of things but punishment for original sin. The Fall taints sexual pleasure and even the innocent sexual organs themselves, now characterized as shameful parts *(pudenda)*. For the Church Fathers, all sexual relations—even the most pure, even those that aim not at the satisfaction of desire but at procreation or fulfillment of the divine will—are sinful, at least by association.[29] For in the heat of action, even the purest intentions are often forgotten. There remains only pleasure, and hateful Lust whispering in our ear that there is no need to wait for the Kingdom of Heaven, that carnal knowledge is not a reminder of the expulsion from the Garden of Eden but its own Garden of Delights, that Paradise is indeed within reach of our hands, our mouths, and our organs—*hic et nunc*, here and now.

The only safe way to avoid the slippery slope of lust is to abstain entirely from sex. This is not easy. Nor, in the eyes of Muslims and Jews, is it desirable. These quarrelsome descendants of Abraham are in agreement on this point: All men are under a religious obligation to found a family and beget children. The righteous are blessed by God with abundant progeny, preferably sons. It is not sexuality in itself that should be avoided, but excess. God gave us those organs for a reason. He expects us to make good use of them. The Wife of Bath would concur: "Tell me to what conclusion or in aid / of what were generative organs made? / And for what profit were those creatures wrought? / Trust me, they cannot have been made for naught."[30]

In the treatise *Yoma* (The Day—i.e., of Kippur), it is recounted that God agreed to put *yetser ha-ra* (the inclination toward evil, or the personalized pleasure principle) into the hands of the sages. But God warned his protégés: "'Realize that if you kill him [the inclination], the world will die out.' They imprisoned him for three days, then looked throughout the land for a [fresh] egg and could not find one. Thereupon they said: 'What shall we do now? Shall we kill him? The world would die out. Shall we beg for half-mercy? They do not grant halves in heaven.' They put out his eyes and let him go."[31] One should not kill Lust, but weaken it—by circumcision, for example, as Rabbi Isaac and Maimonides suggested, or by the Commandments, which are one of the most ambitious programs devised by men to curb desire. Yet with all their great faith in the Commandments, the rabbis remain realistic: "If a man sees that he is overcome by desire (his *yetser*), he should wear black clothes and wrap himself in black covers, and go to a place where he is a stranger among people, and do what his heart desires.[32] It is very important to avoid scandal; and, as in Japanese Kabuki theater, if you wear black you do not exist.

The first Christians were less committed to worldly virtue than the Jews and, later, the Muslims. They were in a hurry to reach the Kingdom of Heaven, and the prospect that humans would not increase and multiply scarcely bothered them.[33] In any case, they were persuaded that the Day of Judgment was near—the Kingdom was at hand. They rejected the prosaic, even humorous, Jewish approach to lust. To them, lust was no joking matter. It was a terrible, dangerous trap that lured men to the world of sin and to its Evil Prince. Yet as time passed and the Kingdom's nearness turned metaphorical, they had to concede that avoiding this deadly trap altogether was beyond the power of most mortals. One has to compromise with the *yetser.* "It is good for a man not to marry," writes Paul. "But since there is so much immorality, each man should have his own wife, and each woman her own husband. . . . I would wish that all men were as I am. But each man has his own gift from God; one has this gift, another has that. Now, to the unmarried and the widows I say: It is good for them to stay unmarried, as I am. But if they cannot control themselves, they should marry, for it is better to marry than to burn with passion."[34]

Over time, Catholics developed a division of labor. Those aspiring to perfection would totally renounce sex and become priests, monks, and nuns. The others would do their best, hoping that God's indulgence and the virtues of their spiritually stronger brothers and sisters would win them seats in the back rows of Paradise. Given their low opinion of desire, the men of the Church proved amenable to surprising compromises. They authorized prostitution and concubinage—moral sewage systems that prevented male desire from overflowing. There was even a certain willingness to treat feminine lust with understanding. Robert de Courçon, a theologian and cardinal of English origin who was chancellor of the University of Paris in the thirteenth century, said that if a woman let it be known to her husband, by word or even by gestures, that she wanted to sleep with him, he should accede to her demand, even on Holy Friday or Easter Day (when sexual relations were in principle forbidden).[35] What good was marriage if it could not pour the relatively cold waters of licit sex on the burning body of a spouse in need?

And what about those who refused to reach a compromise with their bodies? They had to sublimate. Rabbi Ishmael taught: "My son, if this villain [Lust] assails thee, lead him to the schoolhouse."[36] But distraction was not enough. Religion, as we have seen, offered its own erotic frenzy. Mystics of all three monotheistic religions have described God as the object of erotic desire. God is the Beloved referred to in the sacred nuptial Song of Solomon:

> His head is purest gold;
> His hair is wavy and black as a raven.
> His eyes are like doves by the water streams,
> Washed in milk, mounted like jewels.
> His cheeks are like beds of spice yielding perfume,
> His lips are like lilies dripping with myrrh.[37]

And who is the female lover? She is the soul, the heavenly groom's virgin bride. In the spiritual sphere, women are no longer expected to be modest and bashful. Christian female mystics (in Islam female mystics were marginalized, and in Judaism they were altogether silenced) expressed their passion to God, especially God Incarnate, in terms and with a passion that were impermissible toward an earthly object of desire. In the spiritual sphere, the rules of restraint no longer applied; decorum gave way to ecstasy.[38] Life was a battlefield between carnal and spiritual love.

The quest for spiritual ecstasy was not new, of course. In the *Phaedrus*, Plato describes this conflict with a parable. The human soul, he writes, is like a man driving a chariot hitched to two horses. One of these is noble, white, magnificent, and obedient; the other is dark, ugly, and rebellious. One is the rational, the other the carnal impulse. When a man meets a person he loves, his beauty (Plato always posits male objects of desire) fills his soul with excitement.[39] The sight of the lover reminds the charioteer and the spiritual horse of the idea of beauty, which transcends the corporeal and the concrete and draws them up into the spiritual heights of pure forms. Unfortunately the Platonic soul, like Rabbi Isaac's uncircumcised man, has an enemy within its walls: the corporeal horse has other plans.

I remember the wave of desire that violently threw me off my spiritual high horse when I reached puberty. I remember the deep despair that gripped me, the feeling that my flesh was rising up against me. Until my raging hormones changed my life, I had been firmly in control—at least, I thought so. I was a brainy boy forever analyzing and dissecting the world. It all made sense to me. Others were irrational; *I* was not. I was walled securely behind my intellectual fortifications. There was no problem that more books and more thinking could not solve. But suddenly I lost control. Nothing made sense. My body went from being a servant I generally ignored to being a relentless master. Day after day and night after night, women, their bodies, their touch, their odor, filled my dreams. I desperately wanted girls that only the day before I had found silly and boring. But to get their attention, one needed to perform elaborate courting rituals for which I had neither the knowledge nor the skill. My trusted books had no answers. No matter how much I tried to read, I could not rid myself of the images that defied logic and set fire to my loins. In vain, I tried to fight back (I took the recommended cold showers and read more books). Try stopping a flood by sticking your finger in the dam.

The evil horse of the body does not accept the bit with resignation. Disrespectful and impudent, it demands its pound of flesh. Plato thought that the rider should impose his will on the rebellious horse of the flesh. "The effect upon the charioteer is the same as before, but more pronounced; he falls back like a racer from the starting rope, pulls the bit backward ever more violently than before from the teeth of the unruly horse, covers his scurrilous tongue and jaws with blood, and forces his legs and haunches to the ground, causing him much pain. Now, when the bad horse has gone through the same experience many times and has ceased from his unruliness, he is humbled and follows henceforth the bidding of the charioteer, and when he sees the beautiful one, he is overwhelmed with fear."[40] Breaking carnal desire involves violence, Plato believes. It is not easy, but it's possible.

Perhaps. In the *Symposium,* Plato offers an alternative view of carnal love. The participants at the banquet all praise Eros, the god of love. Plato assigns to Aristophanes a speech in praise of physical love. In the beginning, recounts Aristophanes, humans were built like spheres endowed with eight limbs and two heads. These humans were divided into three categories: men, women, and hermaphrodites. These beings possessed enormous force and were very proud of their powers. The gods, in their fear and envy, decided to weaken humans. So Zeus cut each one of them in two, just the way "you would cut a hard-boiled egg with a piece of string." From then on, human beings have been halves, forever looking for their other halves and longing to be reunited with them. The halves who were men are attracted to men, the halves who were women to women, and the halves who were her-maphrodites are each attracted to the opposite sex. Human beings are drawn to each other not just because they seek physical gratification. They are looking for the union that will make them feel whole again, if only for a minute.

> If Hephaestus with his tools were to stand over them as they lay in the same place and were to ask, "What is it that you want, human beings, to get for yourselves from one another?"—and if in their perplexity he were to ask them again, "Is it this you desire, to be with one another in the very same place, as much as is possible, and not to leave one another night and day? For if you desire that, I am willing to fuse you and make you grow together into the same thing, so that—though two—you would become one; and as long as you lived, you would both live together just as though you were one; and when you died, there again in Hades you would be dead together as one instead of as two. So see if you love this and would be content if you got it." We know that there would not be even one who, if he heard

this, would refuse, and it would be self-evident that he wants nothing else than this; and he would quite simply believe he had heard what he had been desiring all along: in conjunction and fusion with the beloved, to become one from two. The cause of this is that this was our ancient nature and we were wholes. So love is the name for the desire and the pursuit of the whole.[41]

For Aristophanes, carnal love is neither vile nor ignoble. It is not an outlet for the base pressures of lust welling up in the body, or a mechanism that produces offspring. It expresses a noble (albeit impossible) longing for wholeness, a wholeness that we lost when we were expelled from the warm body of our mother. Perhaps Freud was right to think that the missing half of every human being is the lost mother of our personal prehistory. Perhaps every partner we find, whether female or male, is only a substitute. But wouldn't it be nicer to think that we are not looking for substitutes? Wouldn't it be nicer to think that we are looking for the real thing, *our* real thing? The Talmud states that "forty days before the creation of a child, a [heavenly voice] issues forth and proclaims: 'The daughter of A is meant for B.'"[42] Perhaps, throughout our lives, we are seeking not transitory pleasures, but that daughter of A or that son of B for whom we are willing to leave father and mother, and with whom we wish to be united so as to become one flesh.[43] Can we find that person in our wanderings from mattress to mattress? Can we ever feel whole again? Probably not, warns the Roman poet Lucretius in *De rerum natura* (The Nature of Things): "Nor can they rub off something from tender limbs with hands wandering aimless all over the body. They cling greedily close together and join their watering mouths and draw deep breaths, pressing teeth on lips. But all is vanity, for they can rub nothing off, nor can they penetrate and be absorbed body in body."[44]

It may be impossible, but the attempt can be fun. It may be more than fun. I would like to call, as witness for the defense, the twelfth-century abbess Heloise. The wise Heloise was cruelly separated from her beloved husband, Pierre Abelard, after he was castrated by her family. In shock, he entered a monastery and asked her to take the veil. She agreed, but even under religious cover she refused to turn her back on past love and past lust. From her convent of the Paraclete, she sent Abelard some of the most powerful love letters ever written. The last word belongs to her.

"The pleasures of lovers which we shared have been too sweet—they can never displease me, and can scarcely be banished from my thoughts. Wherever I turn, they are always there before my eyes, bringing with them awakened longings and fantasies which will not let me sleep. Even during the celebration of the Mass, when our prayers should be purer, lewd visions of those pleasures take such a hold on my unhappy soul that my thoughts are on their wantonness instead of on prayers. I should be groaning over the sins I have committed, but I can only sigh for what I have lost."[45]

GLUTTONY

Gula

The Church considered gluttony one of the sins that lower a human being from the spiritual to the corporeal. The need to relieve hunger is not a sin in itself of course—even though, as we shall see, the Church has high regard for stomachs that growl for the Lord. The sin of gluttony resides not in the fact of eating, but in the eater's state of mind.[1] Gregory the Great formulated it like this: The glutton eats before he's hungry and continues to eat when he is no longer hungry; he craves costly and gratuitously sophisticated dishes; he eats too much and with excessive eagerness; he seeks not sustenance, but pleasure; he becomes the slave of his stomach and of his palate.[2]

This contempt for gluttons is not limited to Christianity. In all cultures, moralists criticize the excess inherent in gluttony, reproaching the glutton for seeking to satisfy his basest needs at the expense of nobler pleasures. In a letter to his mother, Helvia, Seneca rails against gluttons:

> The body's needs are few: it wants to be free from cold, to banish hunger and thirst with nourishment. If we long for anything more, we are exerting ourselves to serve our vices, not our needs. We do not need to scour every ocean, or to

load our bellies with the slaughter of animals, or to pluck shellfish from the unknown shores of the furthest sea. . . . They seek to stock their pretentious kitchens by hunting beyond the Phasis, and they aren't ashamed to ask for birds from the Parthians. . . . From all sides, they collect everything familiar to a fastidious glutton. From the furthest sea is brought food which their stomachs, weakened by a voluptuous diet, can scarcely receive. They vomit in order to eat, and eat in order to vomit, and the banquets for which they ransack the whole world they do not even deign to digest.[3]

For Seneca, Roman gluttony reflects loss of judgment and lack of restraint. Better to invest energy and resources in the development of the mind than to become addicted to bodily pleasures. The Christian critique of the glutton as well as of the gourmet is part of a long tradition of philosophical criticism of ostentatious consumption and intemperance.[4] But for Christians, this "bodily addiction" represents much more. The person who loses the battle against his voracious body loses more than the respect of philosophers. Between the *triclinium* (dining room) and the *latrina,* he may lose his soul. In the cosmic conflict between God and Satan, the mind is allied with God; the body often does the work of Satan. He who serves his stomach cannot serve Christ at the same time: "For as I have often told you before and now say again even with tears, many live as enemies of the cross of Christ. Their destiny is destruction, their god is their stomach, and their glory is in their shame. Their mind is on earthly things."[5]

The Church did not like the pursuit of corporeal happiness, whether it derived from sexual organs, the palate, or the stomach.[6] Not that the body is bad in itself—the Church repudiated the dualism that called upon spiritual men and women to reject the whole material world as evil. The Church taught that matter is not the work not of the

Devil but the work of God, and that the human body is not, from its very creation, a death trap for the soul. When God looked upon his creation, material and spiritual, on the sixth day, he saw that it was "very good." Things have gone awry since that happy day. In the struggle between God and the rebel angel Lucifer, the body is an easier prey than the soul. The body provokes and seduces the soul, inadvertently doing the work of the Tempter. The flesh flaunts its cheap wares before man's willing but wavering spirit. Again and again the flesh leads the spirit astray. In the last act of the drama of sin and redemption, the body will be fully rehabilitated and purified of the Devil's filth. In the Kingdom of Heaven, the righteous will not remain spirits without bodies.[7] They will recover their bodies, which have been healed and transfigured, shining brightly like Christ's body on Mount Tabor.

The body should know its place. In the cosmic order, it is classified below the mind and should remain subordinate to it. So long as it acts like an obedient domestic, there is no evil in it. When it threatens to forget its place and start giving orders, it must be forced by threat and punishment to reassume its yoke. In the war between body and soul, between matter and spirit, pleasure is the most dangerous weapon in the body's arsenal. Pleasure promises Paradise here and now. Oh, impatience! It comes, as the Arab proverb says, from Satan.

If you wish to repulse Satan and do the Lord's will, you must be armed with patience. When pleasure makes its appearance, patience tends to make its exit. Worse, pleasure is addictive. If it is not consumed wisely and responsibly, in small doses, it can be spiritually lethal. The Church Fathers thought that the various kinds of pleasure are all linked to one another, just as, according to today's moralists, soft drugs lead necessarily to hard drugs. The Fathers believed that the pleasures of the table, in particular, lead inexorably to those of the flesh. Then it's but a few steps farther to jealousy, anger, violence, and the spiritual sloth that destroys the soul. Uncontrolled gluttony opens the door to other desires—both because communal meals provide occasions for suppos-edly legitimate meetings between the sexes, and because a full belly gives birth to all sorts of nastiness.[8] The way to a man's heart is through his stomach. Well, perhaps not to his heart exactly.

If you wish to strengthen your soul, weaken your body. To what point? As always, it depends on your objectives and on your ambitions. Are you looking only for minimal assurance of escaping Hell, or do you seek to join the company of the holy martyrs and confessors? The spirit of most people is willing (if not to pursue the good per se, then its ever-lasting reward), but their flesh is weak. If you try to jump too high, you might trip and slide all the way to Hell. "One does not impose a rule on a community unless the majority can abide by it."[9] This wise rule of the sages is a precaution against spiritual ambition. Unless you're a trained athlete, do not try to jump across chasms. Taking the bridge might be less heroic, but it is safer. The average person would do well merely to avoid excess and eat moderately, so as to satisfy his hunger and quench his thirst. This should be enough.

But there are people who want to do more than "enough." Not only do they refuse to worship their stomach; they wish to sentence it to a strict diet—"the bread of adversity and the water of affliction."[10] To satisfy the will of their divine Master, they renounce bodily satisfac-tions; and to fill their hearts, they empty their bellies. These people are not content just to avoid gluttony; they want to use physical mortifica-tion as a battering ram to force open the gates of Heaven. John Cassian, one of the fathers of monasticism in the West, wrote in the fifth cen-tury: "He [Paul] describes himself as one wrestling strenuously with his flesh, and he declares that he has not struck the blow of abstinence against it in vain, but has won the fight by putting his body to death. Now that it has been chastised by the blows of abstinence and struck by the boxing gloves of fasting, he has conferred on his victorious spirit the crown of deathlessness and the palm of incorruption."[11]

Appearing in the East shortly after the end of the Great Persecution (303–313) and the conversion of Emperor Constantine, the ascetic movement aimed at harnessing the body to the chariot of redemption, with the goal of making it, here and now, the purified body of the Resurrection.[12] For this purpose, the Christian ascetic—anchorite or cenobite, hermit or monk—had to pledge total sexual abstinence, renounce all worldly goods, and live in poverty.[13] In a thousand ways, the ascetics deprived their bodies of pleasure, even the most modest. Wearing a hair shirt, they worked outdoors in the implacable sun of the Egyptian desert or in the glacial cold of northern Europe. They denied themselves sleep, and when they did close their eyes, they chose an inhospitable resting place that allowed their bodies little comfort. They rarely washed themselves or the rags that covered their bodies. They gave up laughing; they wore themselves out praying; they practiced long fasts, since fasting feeds the soul. Sometimes they ate nothing for days on end; sometimes they were content with a fistful of dry figs and a sip of scummy water. The nourishment was always insufficient, always tasteless, always without inspiration or sensuality, always leaving them barely satisfied or without any satisfaction at all. "A man leaves the world," say the rabbis, "and not half of his heart's desire is in his hands."[14] The ascetic leaves the world without even a thousandth of his heart's desires.[15] To deprive oneself of food was to deprive oneself of the most basic bodily needs. It was a struggle of culture against nature *and* nurture.

Self-denial was perceived not as an attempt to force the body into subjection, but as a struggle for life or death. It is said that one of the Desert Fathers, Dorotheus, worked without protection or rest in the Egyptian desert during the hottest hours of the day. When asked why he persisted in torturing his miserable body, he replied, "It kills me—I kill it."[16] Other monks flagellated themselves until their body was a bloody mass, tortured themselves by encasing their body in a cuirass of rusty metal (as did Lorenzo Loricato), or even severed pieces of their own flesh (as did Marie d'Oignie).

Saint Francis of Assisi thought that the body did not deserve the title of horse, not even a rebellious and deformed one. He called his body Donkey, in order to show his contempt for it. The patron saint of animals, who showed great compassion for all God's creatures, who preached to birds and greeted wolves as brothers, had little compassion for Donkey. He threw it into thorn bushes, rolled it in the snow, left it naked in the cold of winter, and rarely tended to its many maladies. One day, having suffered from quartan fever, he allowed himself to eat a little meat in broth to try to recover his strength. Immediately he was seized with remorse and ordered his disciples to lead him naked into the central square of Assisi, a cord around his neck. "Here is the glutton," he declares, "who has grown fat on chicken meat."[17]

Toward the end of his life, the unfortunate Donkey collapsed under the yoke. Francis' spirit was strong, but his body was broken. One of the brothers asked the saint the reason for his great cruelty to his body. Had it acted against his will? On the contrary, replied Francis, it always hastened to obey all his orders and commands. "Then where is your generosity, Father?" asked the friar. "Is this how you render evil for good to a friend in need?" "You are right," replied Francis. He asked forgiveness of his body, promising to take better care of it and to give it some joy. "But how could this exhausted body enjoy itself?" comments Thomas de Celano, author of a life of Saint Francis. "How can you sustain that whose parts have collapsed?"[18]

Fasting is strong medicine for maladies of the soul, but its side effects can be almost as dangerous as the sickness itself. The rabbis knew that. They were suspicious of asceticism. Self-denial implies a criticism of the Creator who made us. He gave us food and drink for our enjoyment (there are special blessings for enjoyment—*birkot hanehenin*). Self-denial is always suspect. "In the future, a man shall be required to account for every [good] thing he saw with his eyes and did not eat."[19] Maimonides is very emphatic in his rejection of asceticism, which he deems worse than futile:

A man may say: since envy and lust and pride and their like are vices that remove a man from the world, I shall abstain from them and go to the opposite extreme—thus he will not eat meat or drink wine or marry a woman, or live in a nice dwelling or wear nice clothes, but wear sackcloth and a hair shirt and so on, like the priests of the idolatrous [here referring to Christians]. But this is an evil way, and one must avoid it. And he who walks this way is called a sinner, as it is said concerning the Nazirite: [the priest] is "to make atonement for him because he sinned in the matter of the soul."[20] And if a Nazirite,[21] who abstained only from wine, needs atonement, how much more so he who abstains from each and every thing! Thus, the sages command that a man must abstain only from what the Torah orders him to abstain from, and must not vow to abstain from permitted things. The sages said: "Is not what the Torah has forbidden enough, that you forbid yourself other things?" It follows from this rule that those who always practice asceticism are not acting correctly. The sages did not allow a man to torment himself by fasting. And concerning these things and their like, Solomon has said:[22] "Do not be overrighteous; neither be overwise. Why destroy yourself?"[23]

Even more dangerous than casting aspersions on Creation (the rabbis were not incapable of raising the occasional eyebrow at the world God was so pleased with) was the spiritual damage that asceticism could inflict. The will to struggle against excess can lead to the opposite extreme, and the desire to flee delights can become a source of pleasure, just as the desire to flee honors can become a source of pride—*superbia humilitatis*. The Church Fathers, knowing the pitfalls of an exaggerated zeal for sanctity, as well as the dangers of hypocrisy, tried to impose discipline on bodies *and* souls. Discipline is the best antidote for the overly strong medicine of asceticism. The Rule that Saint Benedict laid down in the sixth century for his monks firmly regulates what a Benedictine monk may eat and in what quantities, so that he neither makes fasting an extreme sport nor indulges in gluttony and drunkenness. The daily regimen consists of two meals—each offering a choice between two dishes, plus a supplement of fresh vegetables (if there are any)—and an allotment of about five hundred grams of bread. If the monks are performing particularly hard work, the abbot can add a little more to this menu. The meals are eaten at fixed hours and under strict surveillance. Even the supplementary ration given to the monks who distribute the food is fixed by the Rule (a slice of bread and a glass of wine).

During seasonal fasts, Benedictine monks eat only a single meal (without meat) every twenty-four hours. They may wish to deprive themselves further, for their own spiritual health and for the greater glory of God. But they may do so only with the approval of the abbot, for "what is done without the authorization of the spiritual father shall be considered as arrogance and boastfulness and not as a merit."[24] A central feature of the Benedictine community is its deep distrust of human nature. Humans are weak and rebellious by nature. They are prone to make bad use of good things. Only by uniting their puny individual forces under the stern guidance of an experienced abbot, by renouncing the idea of distinguishing themselves from the common lot, can monks succeed in attaining the desired degree of sanctity. Sanctity is the result of a collective effort, not an individual race to the finish line.[25]

One does not easily subdue the will to outdo others and win the race to the Kingdom. The abbots might rebuke and punish those who are in too much of a hurry, but each generation has its spiritual athletes who in their haste to reach Heaven leave their companions far behind. In the *Historia Lausiaca*, Palladius mentions such an athlete of asceticism, the hermit Macarius (who died in the year 390). From his arrival in the monastic community of Tabennisi in Egypt, he sought to distinguish himself, to outdo everyone else. "He saw [during Lent] that each monk was practicing asceticism by following a different routine. One ate only in the evening, another every second evening, another every fifth evening. Another remained standing the whole night but sat during the day. Macarius . . . went into a corner. Until the forty days were over and Easter arrived, he did not touch bread or water, did not bend his knee or lie down. He took no nourishment except for a few leaves of cabbage on Sunday, only to give the impression of eating." But the community of Tabennisi was not a loose collection of salvation-seeking hermits. It was a disciplined unit in the Army of the Lord. Its founder, Pachomius (who died in 346), formerly a soldier in the Roman army, initiated the cenobitic, or common, life precisely in order to curb the excesses of men like Macarius. The monks were not impressed by such zeal—or at least, they were not amused. They complained to Abbot Pachomius that Macarius was introducing a spirit of competition and individualism into the community, and asked him to send the undisciplined hunger artist away. Pachomius agreed. He took Macarius to the monastery church, and discovered by divine inspiration that the newcomer was not the anonymous novice but Macarius, the celebrated ascetic. He chased him away with this ironic remark: "Go your way. . . . You have edified us enough."[26]

If eating too much or paying too much attention to what you eat is a sign of gluttony, then not eating at all (or ingesting repugnant, culturally "inedible" fare) is often considered an act of subversion against those in power. The spectacular fasting of Macarius was not perceived by the monks of Tabennisi as a disciplined harnessing of the body to the spirit, but as a hunger strike or, worse, as a thinly veiled challenge to the existing order by an unruly spirit. The terrible violence that the ascetic directed against his own body was an implicit threat, a show of force. It could very easily turn from the ascetic himself to those who held authority. In Benedictine monasteries, the Rule furnished abbots—even those of lower spiritual authority than Saint Pachomius—with powerful institutional means for repressing any threat of subversion. In less disciplined religious communities, the authorities were not so successful.

Catherine of Siena (1347–1380) was a renowned and extremely popular champion of fasting. In 1970 she was declared a Doctor of the Church (one of only three such women, the others being Teresa of Avila and Thérèse of Lisieux). At age sixteen, Catherine entered the order of the *mantellate* ("cape wearers"). This was a Dominican Third Order, whose members did not live in a convent under the strict supervision of an abbess, but instead worked for the needy in the community. When she was twenty-one, Catherine restricted her diet to fresh vegetables, bitter herbs, and water. This was a severe regime, but not sufficient to raise eyebrows. Four years later, however, Catherine had a mystical experience that changed her life. While taking care of a woman with a cancerous breast disease, she was suddenly overcome with disgust at the sight and odor of the diseased flesh.

The bodily horse was rearing its head, and Catherine decided to teach it a lesson. She gathered a ladleful of pus from the lesion, and without paying attention to the sick woman's horrified protests, drank the nauseating liquid. That night, Jesus revealed himself to Catherine in a vision. He invited her to drink the blood of redemption from his pierced side. From that moment, she said, she had no need of earthly nourishment, which in any case she couldn't digest. She ate nothing but the Host—the flesh and blood of Christ.[27]

The consumption of bodily secretions arouses strong revulsion in us. This revulsion is not natural, but cultural. Infants have no problem eating their feces or their vomit, just as adults in certain societies are not revolted by swallowing semen or drinking blood. Secretions are cultural markers. By consuming them, one crosses a symbolic threshold from a culture into "outer darkness," where no self-respecting human dwells. The forced consumption of bodily secretions often constitutes an act of extreme degradation, pushing the victim beyond the boundaries of the human. Saint Catherine's voluntary consumption of pus was an act of power. It showed that she had overcome her own repugnance, while provoking disgust in others. She proclaimed herself above the norms. Her behavior marked her as unpredictable. Her total abstinence from nourishment (let us set aside the question of what was "really" happening and how she survived without eating) was seen as presenting a religious and moral dilemma. Was Catherine possessed by God or by the Devil? It was not easy to say. The ecclesiastical authorities were unhappy. The Church loves clarity. They ordered Catherine to eat. Asceticism by the rules was one thing; total abstinence from all food was something else. Even Christ had fasted for no more than forty days. This was a victory not over gluttony, but over humanity. Catherine was a human being. She was expected to behave like one.

For the remainder of her life, the saint waged an incessant struggle against the authorities. They ordered: "Eat or you will die!" She replied: "I cannot. Eating kills me. If I must die, it's better to die of hunger than from overeating." Each attempt to force Catherine to eat provoked serious bodily and mental reactions in her. She simply wouldn't, couldn't, do as she was told. And what about the sacred virtue of obedience? What would this obedient daughter of the Church do if Jesus Himself reappeared in her visions, encouraging her to persevere and threatening her critics with dire punishments? (She faithfully reported her visions, including the threats, to friend and foe.) In the end, they left her alone. She died at thirty-three.[28]

Catherine's stubborn refusal to eat brings to mind the behavior of modern girls suffering from anorexia nervosa. In the book *Holy Anorexia*, Rudolph Bell maintains that many of the saintly hunger strikers of the past were in fact anorexics.[29] This conclusion is problematic. First, it is not always evident that these saints were really abstaining from all food. A number of them claimed to have eaten nothing but the Host for years, yet they did not become the walking skeletons that we see in food-disorder clinics, nor, it seems, were they in particularly bad health. Theresa Neumann, for example, the fasting woman of Konnersreuth (1898–1962), was, to judge by her photographs, quite chubby. Unless professional historians are allowed to believe in miracles, it would seem that these women were filling their need for proteins and carbohydrates one way or another. Moreover, the motivations of the saintly fasting women and modern anorexics are quite different: the former were totally indifferent to their bodily appearance; the latter live and die for it.[30]

But the two groups do have something in common. The refusal to eat is often a declaration of independence—a symbolic assertion of autonomy and autarchy. Such declarations provoke all kinds of anxious responses. The religious authorities ordering Saint Catherine to eat were worried that a person who declared herself free of the laws of nature could not be expected to pay much attention to rules and regulations. The concerned mother running after her child with a banana is worried that unless her children eat "properly," she will be considered a bad mother (by others, but also by herself). Prelates and mothers, through their anxious reaction to the refusal to take food, reveal their weakness to those under their authority. A stubborn hunger strike that does not yield to sanctions, to threats of violence, or even to actual violence, realigns the structures of familial power. In the family of the young anorexic, everything revolves around the hunger striker. Food—the primordial human currency—becomes a family obsession. Whether she (the majority of anorexics are female) intends this or not, her parents interpret her eating as a favor to them and her fasting as their punishment. Whatever they do, so long as the anorexic continues to put her life at risk, it is *she* who is the center of attention. The hunger striker is supposedly fasting to cure herself of gluttony, but in fact she has much in common with the person guilty of that deadly sin. Both are obsessively focused on the body.[31] Both derive pleasure from the belly.

Nowadays, men and women in the West are for the most part quite free of the idea that there is something sinful about the flesh. We no longer see the body as an obstacle. Quite the opposite: the body has become the privileged center of our being.[32] It has to be pampered, indulged, spruced up. It requires high maintenance. Never have so many products been sold for bodily care; never have people made so much effort to offer the body oblations and burnt offerings, with no pangs of conscience and at great expense. The body has been liberated. As it turns out, however, this liberation from old guilts has given rise to new ones. The new, liberated Western body has become a master that often proves more exacting than the medieval soul. Modern society is trying to regularize the body, just as premodern society tried to regularize the soul—with strict standards of orthodoxy and with threats of eternal damnation. The liberated body must be chiseled, healthy, shaped according to canons set by those who control mass consumption and public opinion. Producing standardized commodities saves money and effort. We should therefore develop bodies that look good in the clothing that fashion dictates, and subscribe to the sexual fantasies manufactured by the dream industry. We punish our bodies for their own good. Under the scalpels of plastic surgeons, in gyms, sports clubs, and dieting groups, we serve and adore our bodies. We sweat; we forgo the foods that we love; we do without the rest that our bodies desire. Liberation of the body is hard work.

It is also difficult for those who do not have the strength or the ability to produce a healthy body and shapely curves. They carry their BMI, or body mass index—the new formula by which sins of the flesh are calculated—as evidence of their weak will and undisciplined appetite. According to the OECD, more than half of all people in the United States, the United Kingdom, and Australia are overweight.[33] It is estimated that Americans alone spend between $22 billion and $55 billion per year on weight-loss products. Dieting is a Sisyphean process. You lose and you gain *ad infinitum* and *ad nauseam*. Think of the happy days when getting thinner was considered unfortunate and gaining weight was seen as good. And the sad thing about this new gluttony and its flipside, the new antigluttony, is that they bring little joy. People who stuff themselves with fast food, snacks, and chocolate bars rarely do so for the delights of the palate. They eat out of loneliness and fear; they eat in the hope of regaining the sense of comfort and security that we all lost when we were weaned of our mother's milk. Food is the most primitive anti-anxiety drug. In our anxiety-ridden society, food has become an addiction.[34]

So today a flat stomach is the gateway to earthly paradise; a bulging belly, the surest way to social hell. In past centuries, bellies were not that important; still, Heaven and Hell were associated with food and with food metaphors. It is worth recalling the menus that the faithful of the three monotheistic religions could look forward to in the afterlife. Righteous Jews could expect dishes of Wild Ox and Leviathan. They would be offered wine made from the vines of the seven days of Creation; rivers of milk, wine (of more recent vintage), persimmon juice, and honey would be at their disposal. As for evildoers, Rabbi Yehoshua ben Levi recounts that in Hell he saw "men feeding on their own flesh, others eating burning coals, others devoured alive by worms. [He saw] men who were fed by force on fine sand and whose teeth broke. And God (Hallowed Be His Name) said to them: 'Wicked men, when you were eating your plunder, it was sweet in your mouths. Now, you no longer have the stomach for it?'"[35]

Righteous Muslim men, when they are not occupied in the agreeable company of the lovely virgins that are reserved for them, will eat fruits of all kinds and drink from a pure and delicious alcoholic spring that will never make them drunk. They will also enjoy four rivers, of water that is never tainted, milk that never goes sour, delectable wine, and pure honey. The wicked will eat the fruit of Zaqqum, which is bitter, like absinthe. "It grows in the nethermost part of Hell, bearing fruit like devils' heads. On it they shall feed and with it they shall cram their bellies, together with draughts of scalding water."[36]

And Christians? Their saints in Heaven will neither eat nor drink (except perhaps the flesh and blood of Christ). But the souls of the damned in Hell will profit from a rich menu. Some will consume their own flesh or that of their companions-in-torment; others will swallow various repulsive dishes—frogs, serpents, lizards, filth, mud, excrement, urine, and vomit (their own). Some will be fed by devils and others will suffer atrocious hunger—a punishment for their gluttony during life. In sum: the hellish menu is extremely varied, but the quality of the food is awful. The menu offered in Paradise is very monotonous, but of higher quality. As for the service, there's no comparison.

A third possibility is the Land of Cockaigne, which according to medieval legend is an earthly paradise where gluttony is fully justified and vindicated. The Land of Cockaigne does not obey the orders of the rabbinic courts or the rules of the Roman Catholic Church. It is a peasants' dreamland, a country where no work is required, where leisure is endless and guiltless, where food and drink are abundant, where fried chickens and roast pigs carry themselves to the mouths of lazy eaters. In the Land of Cockaigne, overeating does not damage one's health, and nobody worries about a few extra pounds.[37]

After our long tour through the regions of guilt-ridden eating and power-hungry fasting, Cockaigne brings us back to simpler pleasures. I would like to end this chapter with a brief account of guiltless gluttony. My son Daniel was a very fussy eater as a boy. He was a skinny vegetarian who had to be reminded to eat. When he hit puberty, all this changed. He started eating unbelievable quantities of food and getting taller almost by the hour. Soon he felt that vegetarianism was for sissies and that I, as his father, must feed him real food—namely, meat. I agreed. We went to my favorite steakhouse and he ordered the biggest steak on the menu—two and a half pounds of prime beef. He began devouring the bloody bovine flesh with total concentration. His hands and his jaws moved in perfect harmony. I watched him with admiration. After about two pounds of the steak had vanished, he raised his eyes from his plate, looked at me, and said: "Dad, I am very happy."

7

GREED
Avaritia

It is strange that greed should figure in the shortlist of super-sins. Rather than being a distinct vice, greed seems to be a specific type of covetousness. Greed is motivated by envy, the desire to possess what belongs to another. In most cases, greed is a means and not an end in itself. "Money," Max Weber assures us, "is the most abstract and 'impersonal' element that exists in human life."[1] It is impossible to eat it, impossible to drink it, impossible to have sex with it. But one can eat, drink, and buy sexual pleasure *with* it. When your money is "good," those little metal disks and paper rectangles that are worth practically nothing in themselves become omnipotent, conjuring up everything we desire.[2]

Popular sayings testify to the magical force of money: Money talks; money makes the world go round; money purifies bastards;[3] in modern societies, money is the ultimate measuring rod—not only of commodities but of each and every thing. One might say that money transforms everything—objects, people, emotions, the gods themselves—into a commodity. What are things worth? They are worth their price on the market, in hard cash. If you do not have money, you are either a saint (that is to say, you have voluntarily chosen to renounce money) or a fool (a loser who does not know how to make money)—or both.

Greed almost always functions as a means for satisfying other desires that are more powerful and more fundamental. You want to accumulate riches to augment your pleasures, your confidence, your status. You want to obtain the right to command others—for, as the Hebrew proverb goes, "it is the opinion of him who has a hundred coins that counts." It is better not to irritate the person whose pockets are full: "Even in your bedroom do not curse the rich, because the bird of the sky may carry your words, and the winged fowl may report what you say."[4] The flattery with which the rich are permanently surrounded is like a warm blanket on a cold day.

But sometimes flattery, comfort, and power are not enough. Sometimes, no matter how much you hoard, the feeling of satiety remains out of reach. For the truly avaricious, greed is insatiable. "Whoever loves money never has money enough."[5] Avarice sometimes ceases to be an instrument and becomes an end in itself. Money, the means of attaining that which we desire, can become the object of our desire.

In the Middle Ages, the usurer incarnated greed. Usurers neither sowed nor harvested; they neither built nor did an honest day's work. They were preoccupied only with money and the profits born from money, not from labor.[6] They refused to lend to their needy brothers out of Christian charity, as the Bible orders. Furthermore, they tried to turn time into a commodity—for interest is paid for no other reason than the passing of time. Money becomes the center of the usurer's universe—more important than friendship, more important than love, more important than saving his body or even his soul. Seized with an irrepressible lust for money, the miser is not ready to give up his cash for the sake of the afterlife. The theologian and inquisitor Etienne de Bourbon (thirteenth century) relates an encounter with such a stubborn usurer that he personally observed.

Here is what I saw with my own eyes. When I was a young student in Paris, I went to the church of the Holy Virgin one Saturday to attend vespers. I saw a man being carried on a stretcher, suffering from a limb burned with the evil that is called the "sacred evil," or the "infernal evil" [ergotism]. He was surrounded by a crowd. People close to him acknowledged that he was a usurer. And so the priests and clerics exhorted him to give up that trade and to promise that he would return his usurious gains, so that the Holy Virgin would deliver him of his illness. But he did not want to listen to them, paying no attention either to criticism or to flattery. At the end of vespers, he persisted in his obstinacy, although this fire had spread all over his body, which had become black and swollen up, and although his eyes were bulging. He was thrown out of the church like a dog, and he died on the spot, that very evening, of that fire, still stubbornly obstinate.[7]

One can interpret this story in different ways. The usurer refused to listen to the priests and clerics either because he did not see anything reprehensible in his occupation, or because he did not believe that in distributing his goods he would be cured of his malady. He was probably right. Ergotism—Saint Anthony's Fire or the "burning sickness"— attacked the righteous just as frequently as it attacked evildoers. There is no sound statistical evidence proving that ergotism responds to charity. Of course, clerics promise us that charity will save us from death, but often reality testifies to the contrary. The health of usurers is better than that of the poor, who shall inherit the Kingdom of Heaven. Usurers have the best doctors, as well as free time and money to frequent gyms. As for mold-infected rye (the main cause of ergotism), it landed more often on the tables of the blameless poor than on those of their

GREED

blameworthy but affluent neighbors. What good would it do a man if he distributed his children's inheritance to the poor in the vain hope of receiving aid from the blessed Virgin Mary?

Etienne de Bourbon was certainly aware of all this. Medieval inquisitors were neither naïve idealists nor particularly credulous. They were practical men of the world who had seen a thing or two in their lives. Etienne was telling didactic stories that were meant to scare sinners into repentance. In real life, inquisitors kept their gunpowder dry even when they prayed ardently to the Mother of God. Yet, seasoned in worldly affairs as they were, these inquisitors were also believing Christians. Whatever they thought about the chances of a last-minute intervention by the Virgin, they could not be very sympathetic to dying usurers. For the Holy Scriptures take a very problematic position on greed. Christ was quite clear about it: "No one can serve two masters. Either he will hate the one and love the other, or he will be devoted to the one and despise the other. You cannot serve both God and Mammon [Money]."[8] For Jesus, money, more than sex or food, is the great enemy of the soul. Money is the Devil, and its servants are Devil worshipers.

Of course, the entire material world is an obstacle on the path to the Kingdom of Heaven. As we saw in previous chapters, the pleasures of the table and the delights of the flesh may lead a man, kicking and screaming with joy, into Hell. But Jesus hates money more than the pleasures of the flesh. The Gospels describe Jesus eating, drinking, and even complaining about the criticism of the more ascetically minded: "For John came neither eating nor drinking, and they say, 'He has a demon.' The Son of Man came eating and drinking, and they say, 'Here is a glutton and a drunkard, a friend of tax collectors and sinners.'"[9] As for women, Jesus is described several times as letting women approach Him and even touch Him, without inquiring about their physical state (were they pure or impure?) or their moral state (were they modest daughters of Israel, or sinners?). On the contrary, when an adulterous woman is brought to Him, and the scribes and Pharisees want to stone her, Jesus defends her by saying: "If any of you is without sin, let him be the first to throw a stone at her."[10] When nobody volunteers, He sends the woman away without punishment or blame: "Woman, where are they? Has no one condemned you?" "No one, sir," she said. "Then neither do I condemn you," Jesus declared. "Go now and sin no more."[11]

Jesus was neither a glutton nor a libertine, but He seems to have viewed gluttony and lust with a certain compassion. It is different with greed. "Blessed are you who are poor, for yours is the kingdom of God. . . . But woe to you who are rich, for you have already received your comfort."[12] In one of His parables, Jesus tells the story of two men, one rich and the other a poor man named Lazarus. The nameless rich man was "clothed in purple and fine linen and fared sumptuously every day." The beggar Lazarus sat at his gate, hoping to pick up the crumbs which fell from the rich man's table, and the dogs came and licked his sores. When the two die, the angels take poor Lazarus to the bosom of Abraham; the rich man is thrown into Hell. Now the rich man begs Abraham to send Lazarus to dip his finger in water to cool the rich man's tongue, but Abraham refuses. He does not accuse the rich man of having sinned, but simply declares: "Son, remember that in your lifetime you received your good things, while Lazarus received bad things, but now he is comforted here and you are in agony."[13] For Jesus, the simple fact of enjoying affluence in this world costs the rich man his salvation. Wealth itself—and not necessarily the sins it brings—is an almost insurmountable obstacle to salvation.

Jesus is not content with parables that one might interpret in various ways. In a famous scene from the Gospel of Matthew, He speaks directly and openly. One day a young man approaches Him and asks what he must do to gain eternal life. At first, Jesus makes a response that would not sound surprising coming from the mouth of a rabbi of his time: "If you want to enter into life, keep the commandments. . . . You shall not murder, You shall not commit adultery, You shall not steal, You shall not bear false witness, Honor your father and mother, and You shall love your neighbor as yourself."[14] Notice that Jesus has removed from this list the Commandments concerning people's relations with God, and has added a commandment to love one's neighbor that does not figure in the Ten Commandments. But the questioner is not content with this answer. Jesus' advice is about the minimum requirement for gaining salvation. But this man wants to attain moral *perfection*. "'All these things I have kept from my youth,' the young man said. 'What do I still lack?' Jesus said to him: 'If you want to be perfect, go, sell what you have and give to the poor and you will have treasure in heaven. Then come, follow me.'"[15] This answer, which does not allow the man to make do with giving alms from his surplus but requires him to renounce all his goods, was not, it seems, what our aspiring perfectionist wanted to hear: "But when the young man heard that saying, he went away sorrowful, for he had great possessions. Then Jesus said to his disciples, 'Assuredly I say to you, that it is hard for a rich man to enter the kingdom of heaven. And again I say to you, it is easier for a camel to go through the eye of a needle than for a rich man to enter the kingdom of God.'"[16]

Few camels succeed in passing through the eye of a needle. So are there no rich people in the Kingdom of Heaven? Not quite. In Luke the Kingdom of Heaven belongs to the "poor." In the Gospel according to Matthew, it belongs to the "poor in spirit."[17] It seems that there were conflicting traditions about the opening words of the Sermon on the Mount. Somehow Matthew's formula sounded better. Now poverty "in spirit" and plain poverty are two totally different things, just as fancy *pain de campagne* is different from simple peasant bread. As we shall see, the rich are much better equipped to be "poor in spirit." The Christian Paradise is full of very rich people who were at the same time poor in spirit to the highest degree.

And what about the sinners, prostitutes, carpenters, and tax collectors who followed Jesus and whom He promised to lead to Heaven?

Those "last who would be first"? Their access is not totally blocked, of course, but their chances are apparently not very good.

How did this spiritual sleight of hand come about? As always, one can blame circumstances—original sin, human nature, history. When you have little, it's easy to give it all to the poor. When you have great possessions, giving them away seems suddenly rather irresponsible. In the beginning, Christianity was the religion of the "last"—of those, like Jesus, whose kingdom was not of this world. During its first three centuries, Christianity was a marginal and persecuted religion that viewed this world and its temptations with contempt and disdain. The model of religious fellowship was that of the ancient apostolic community in Jerusalem, where private property was banned and where wealth flowed "from each according to his ability, to each according to his needs."

But at the start of the fourth century, this situation underwent a fundamental transformation. Constantine the Great abrogated the anti-Christian laws and converted to Christianity. Then, under his heirs, Christianity ceased being one more tolerated religion and became the state religion of the Roman Empire.[18] In the preceding three centuries, men and women had joined the Christian community despite persecution and mortal danger. After the conversion of Constantine, many turned to the baptismal font because of the immense advantages it offered. It did not take long for the persecuted to learn the many advantages of persecution. Stubborn infidels were invited to join the true faith by Christian warriors offering promises of the Kingdom of Heaven with one hand and brandishing the sharp sword of worldly power with the other.[19] What would the crucified Messiah—turning His cheek to those who struck Him—have thought about this? Those who followed in his footsteps rarely paused to ask themselves.

The radical transformation of the Church's status required an equally radical change in its relation to earthly power. Distinguishing between the things that were God's and the things that were Caesar's became increasingly difficult. The Roman emperor (and the rulers of the kingdoms established on the ruins of the Roman Empire) did not consider themselves enemies of Christianity, bent on destroying its ideals; they were defenders of the faith. Secular rulers defended the faith in their customary fashion. As for the Church, it involved itself more and more in the laws of the State, and in mandating respect for those laws. Now even the successors of the apostles recognized that man would eat his neighbor raw without those laws.[20] The Church hastened to sanction within the Christian State what it had reviled in the pagan state. Violence in the service of the community (service whose limits were of course very elastic) went from being blameworthy to being sacred. Holy wars and just wars, the persecution of heretics, apostates, and witches by stern pastors and holy inquisitors, those enthusiastic seekers of error—the love of God made it all kosher.[21]

Newly baptized in the waters of worldly power, the Church legitimized political greed—greed in the service of community. Without Mammon, there is no political power. The machinery of power costs money. Civil servants, soldiers, and lawyers have to be paid. You must have tax collectors. The Church, therefore, announced that one *could* serve two masters—God *and* Mammon. By marvelous means, pastors tried to convince their flock that their wealth was illusory, that the Church's poverty in spirit canceled its earthly riches, that it inherited both the earthly kingdom and the Kingdom of Heaven.[22]

Unlike Christianity, Judaism and Islam did not have any problem with the use of force, or with money. The self-proclaimed descendants of Abraham saw violence as a blameless necessity, and material success—children and wealth—as a sign of God's grace. "He who separates the sacred from the profane will wipe out our sins; He will multiply our offspring and our money like the sand, like the stars in the sky."[23] The Jewish sages were also quite skilled at spiritualizing the Scriptures. They were quick to nullify commandments such as *shmita* (abrogation of debts in the seventh year) and *yovel* (redistribution of land in jubilee years). Property is sacred, and the rich are very sensitive people.[24] Remember Ecclesiastes' advice: "Even in your bedroom do not curse the rich, because the bird of the sky may carry your words, and the winged fowl may report what you say."

Despite Christians' great enthusiasm and skill in extracting spiritual meaning from straight talk, they found things much more complicated. This was partly a matter of timing. When they took control of earthly power, their worldview was already well established. They tried to obscure the message of the Gospels under a thick whitewash of commentary. But the paint peeled, revealing older messages: "For we brought nothing into the world, and we can take nothing out of it. But if we have food and clothing, we will be content with that. People who want to get rich fall into temptation and a trap and into many foolish and harmful desires that plunge men into ruin and destruction. For the love of money is a root of all kinds of evil. Some people, eager for money, have wandered from the faith and pierced themselves with many griefs."[25] These words from the Letter to Timothy are only too explicit. All the commentaries in the world cannot obscure their meaning. Christianity suffers from an irreparable internal rupture between its ascetic pretensions and its powerful attraction to realpolitik, between God and Caesar. After the conversion of Constantine, the Church had judiciously chosen what belonged to Caesar.[26] From time to time, while the ecclesiastical authorities were singing the praises of poverty, people appeared who asserted that Jesus' words were perfectly clear and required no commentary. "Blessed are you who are poor, for yours is the kingdom of God. . . . But woe to you who are rich, for you have already received your comfort."[27] Let us be poor, then.

The monastic movement offered the Christian community a group of highly trained professional ascetics who took a solemn vow of poverty. The professionally poor produced more merit than was necessary for their own salvation. The surplus produced by the holy could nourish the masses of unholy Christians. Exempted from the duty of personal poverty thanks to the holy men and women in the monasteries and convents, the rest could accumulate wealth and fill their coffers with silver and gold.[28] So long as they paid their tithes and offered generous donations to the Church, so long as they made their wealth honorably (from plunder if they were lords; from hard work if they were peasants), they were fine.

In the twelfth century, things began to change. For the first time in centuries the West started producing a surplus of earthly goods. Warmer climate, stronger central government, improved agricultural techniques, growing population—all combined to spur a period of economic growth that lasted about three hundred years. Western society produced more than it could consume. Markets and fairs appeared everywhere. Money reemerged. A new class—the so-called middle class—entered the European stage, never again to leave it. Merchants made their living by questionable means. They profited from other people's hard labor. They made money that begat money. They needed credit and they charged interest. There was nothing subtle or euphemistic about their service to Mammon. They were usurers and money-grubbers. The Church chastised them for their greed: they were uncouth *nouveaux riches*. But as usual, the Church compromised.

The thirteenth century brought a serious spiritual and political challenge that threatened to undo the Catholic compromise.[29] Francesco Bernardone, the founder of the Franciscan order (officially known as the order of Friars Minor), was the son of a prosperous merchant of Assisi. When he was in his twenties he went through a profound moral crisis—a sudden disgust with wealth that only a merchant's son who both admired and hated his father could experience. Francesco, or Francis, was no heretic. He did not question the Church or its wealth. Like his divine role model, he wanted to render unto the new Caesars what was theirs. The end of the world would in any case not be long in coming, and then the Judge would know His own. All that "the poor little man" *(il poverello)* wanted was to save his soul and that of his disciples. Francis wanted to gain this salvation through holy poverty, *sancta paupertas*. Remember Christ's advice to the spiritually ambitious young man: "Sell what you possess and give it to the poor." Francis wanted to do just that, literally. Take no care for tomorrow. Have faith in the Lord. Unlike other monastic orders, whose members were individually poor but extremely wealthy as organizations, the Franciscans had an obligation to live in individual *and* collective poverty, to own nothing except for the shirts on their backs. They were strictly forbidden even to touch money. To survive, they went begging from door to door.

The friars of the first generation of the Franciscan order refused to interpret the Gospels metaphorically. Christ was not speaking to theologians or to literary critics. He was addressing day laborers and prostitutes. His words had to be taken at face value. Franciscans lived in abject poverty. They wandered from place to place, and spread the Good Tidings: "Happy are the poor." Often they slept with empty stomachs, without a roof above their heads. Rumor of them spread in the towns and villages of Europe. Men of the Church living in poverty! The success of the order was immense, almost miraculous. The Franciscan order seemed, at long last, to heal the internal rupture of Christianity, to assuage the spiritual heartburn from which the Church had suffered since the fourth century. The Franciscans were the great hope, the worthy heirs of the Messiah and His apostles, the avant-garde who would lead society as a whole toward the Kingdom of Heaven.[30]

It failed, of course. Even within the lifetime of the order's holy founder, the members of one faction opted for a moral compromise that would allow them to better serve the community. They interpreted the Franciscan Rule a little more spiritually, so they could live much more comfortably. The papacy, which regarded the Franciscans' extreme sanctity like a thorn in its side, aided these brothers to become less holy and less poor. The goods of the order were declared the property of the Church, a stratagem which allowed Franciscans "to have without possessing." This was a very civilized form of poverty. The Friars Minor also made an appeal for a sort of "Sabbath *goy*,"[31] a special agent who took care of their finances so they could abstain from directly touching money. Despite all this rule-bending and compromise, the Franciscans' spiritual pretensions were like a red flag in front of their rivals' noses. The Franciscans were certain (explicitly or tacitly) of being the only true heirs of Christ. The other claimants to the heritage were ultimately imposters, since only the order of Friars Minor obeyed Jesus' commandment by living in holy poverty.[32]

In the fourteenth century, Pope John XXII decided to put an end to this holy game. In a series of papal bulls, the Vicar of Christ decreed that the Franciscans' claim to be the only ones imitating Christ "to the letter" was false and harmful to the soul, that the goods kept for the friars by the Church truly and fully belonged to them, and that Jesus Himself had not lived in absolute poverty. Poverty was not the sole criterion for salvation, but one ascetic practice among many others. Poverty mattered, but not as much as obedience.[33]

Some Franciscans considered such a doctrine unbearable, feeling that it shook the very ground beneath their feet. Others believed in having both feet on the ground of reality and accepted the new law. The former seceded, denouncing the pope as the Antichrist and the Roman Church as the "Great Whore of Babylon." The struggle went on for a hundred years. Much ink, sweat, and even some blood were spilled. At the end of the day, the great Franciscan dream ended in a fiasco. The Franciscan order today is no different from other orders.

The failure of the Franciscan order was much more than an episode of internal ecclesiastical politics. It was a true spiritual earthquake, followed by a tsunami of disappointment that spread across Europe. In the struggle between God and Mammon, Mammon had won—again. The attempt to reinvigorate the Christian world had failed, collapsing under the weight of reality. If shunning worldly goods is unrealistic, let's be greedy and avaricious.

This is what the Protestants did in the sixteenth century. Of course they did not condone greed as such, but they certainly had no taste for poverty. For them, poverty did not procure salvation; it did more harm than good. The God of Luther and Calvin did not love the poor. Poverty was an expression of laziness. Beggars (even when they are called Mendicants) are a burden on society, not a spiritual service to it. God does not love rituals and endless praise. He expects work devoted to His greater glory, not idle talk. Protestants disbanded the monastic orders and drastically reduced the number of public holidays. Work is good, and making money work is even better. Max Weber has shown this well in his famous book *The Protestant Ethic and the Spirit of Capitalism.*[34] Those who wanted "to remain in the contest"— Protestants, Catholics, and Jews—had to adapt to the new rules of the game: hard work, saving, investment. God does not hate the prosperous. Forget about Lazarus and his unfortunate neighbor. Consider instead Christ's parable of the talents. A certain man travels to a far country. He calls his three servants and gives five talents to the first, two to the second, and a single talent to the third.

> Then he who had received the five talents went and traded with them, and made another five talents. And likewise he who had received two gained two more also. But he who had received one went and dug in the ground, and hid his lord's money. [When the lord returned] he who had received five talents came and brought five other talents, saying, "Lord, you delivered to me five talents; look, I have gained five more talents besides them." His lord said to him, "Well done, good and faithful servant." . . . He also who had received two talents came and said, "Lord, you delivered to me two talents; look, I have gained two more talents besides them." His lord said to him, "Well done, good and faithful servant." . . . Then he who had received the one tal-

ent came and said, "Lord, I knew you to be a hard man, reaping where you have not sown, and gathering where you have not scattered seed. And I was afraid, and went and hid your talent in the ground. Look, there you have what is yours." But his lord answered and said to him, "You wicked and lazy servant, you knew that I reap where I have not sown, and gather where I have not scattered seed. So you ought to have deposited my money with the bankers, and at my coming I would have received back my own with interest. So take the talent from him, and give it to him who has ten talents. For to everyone who has, more will be given, and he will have abundance; but from him who does not have, even what he has will be taken away."[35]

Use your talents wisely. Invest—go to the bankers and receive your money back with interest, take risks, reap where you have not sown. To everyone who has, more will be given. From him who does not have, even what he has will be taken away. How sweet it sounds, the word of God. What did Christ mean? It is all a matter of interpretation, of course. Obviously the dying usurer we met at the beginning of the chapter was living in the wrong interpretive environment.

But interpretive environments change. Ultimately, a theory that liberated avarice from any culpability and from any risk of metaphor (for who knows what Christ meant by his parable) was found. In the eighteenth century, Adam Smith—in hindsight, perhaps the most important (if not the most profound) thinker of his age—legitimized self-interest. In his seminal book *The Wealth of Nations*, Smith transformed the providential hand of God into an ensemble of individual egotisms working, by mysterious ways, for the good of the collectivity:

> It is only for the sake of profit that any man employs a capital. . . . He will always, therefore, endeavor to employ it in the support of that industry of which the produce is likely

GREED

to be of the greatest value. . . . He generally, indeed, neither intends to promote the public interest, nor knows how much he is promoting it. By preferring the support of domestic to that of foreign industry, he intends only his own security; and by directing that industry in such a manner as its produce may be of the greatest value, he intends only his own gain, and he is in this, as in many other cases, led by an invisible hand to promote an end which was no part of his intention. Nor is it always the worse for the society that it was no part of it. By pursuing his own interest, he frequently promotes that of the society more effectually than when he really intends to promote it.[36]

When Adam Smith met William Pitt the Younger, the prime minister of Great Britain, the latter declared: "Mister Smith, we are all your disciples." Even today, we are all his disciples, perhaps his too-talented disciples. Smith is the prophet of the free-market economy, and it is the free-market economy and not Christianity (surely not the Christianity of Jesus) that constitutes the real religion of the West today. This religion has its priests, shrines, sacred altars, and missionaries. It goes further than its founder (one wonders if Adam Smith would have approved of Milton Friedman). It is the most successful religion in modern times, and since the collapse of its rival Church—Communism—it has been spreading rapidly over the surface of the globe. Avarice is no longer "the source of all evil": it has become the ultimate virtue.[37] To act for one's personal benefit is to perform an act of charity toward society.[38]

In a scene from the 1987 film *Wall Street*, Gordon Gekko (played by Michael Douglas) declares: "The point is, ladies and gentlemen, that greed—for lack of a better word—*is good*. Greed is right. Greed works. Greed clarifies, cuts through, and captures the essence of the evolutionary spirit. Greed, in all of its forms—greed for life, for money, for love, knowledge—has marked the upward surge of mankind. And greed—you mark my words—will not only save Teldar Paper, but that other malfunctioning corporation called the USA."

Gekko is the bad guy with all the good lines. We don't like the term "greed," though—it's too biblical. How about "entrepreneurial spirit"? Better, isn't it?

The free market is a religion whose priests dominate public opinion. As with all religions, there are some disagreeable facts: the pie is certainly growing bigger, but more and more people are, like Lazarus, eating only the crumbs. The enormous power of money is a genuine threat to democracy and justice. As with all religions, disagreeable facts are rejected out of hand as heresy or folly or both. It is not easy to oppose these vast impersonal forces, but it is dangerous for one's soul to be carried away by their rhetoric into an exaggerated optimism (like any religion, this one promises that Paradise is just around the corner). One must stop from time to time and ask irreverent questions. The invisible hand of this new incarnation of greed is already in your pockets. Be careful you do not find it around your neck.

ANGER

Ira

The West's greatest epic, the *Iliad,* opens with anger, the rage of Achilles:

> Rage—Goddess, sing the rage of Peleus' son Achilles,
> murderous, doomed, that cost the Achaeans countless
>   losses,
> hurling down to the House of Death so many sturdy souls,
> great fighters' souls, but made their bodies carrion,
> feasts for dogs and birds,
> and the will of Zeus was moving toward its end.
> Begin, Muse, when the two first broke and clashed,
> Agamemnon lord of men and brilliant Achilles.[1]

Affront and anger dominate the entire plot. The story begins with a seemingly minor affair: the Trojan priest of Apollo, Chryseis, arrives in the Greek camp with a huge ransom to buy back his daughter. The leader of the Greek armies, King Agamemnon, refuses the request and humiliates the old man. In profound distress, the priest turns to Apollo, who erupts in anger. The god strikes the Greeks with a plague. After they have endured nine days of suffering and death, Achilles calls an assembly and proposes asking the gods why they are punishing the Greeks. Calchas, "the clearest by far of all the seers,"[2] learns the cause. Apollo is angry, he announces, because Agamemnon has disgraced the god's priest. The soothsayer's words inflame Agamemnon: "furious, his dark heart filled to the brim, blazing with anger now, his eyes like searing fire."[3] Seething with rage, Agamemnon is willing to give up the girl, but only on the condition that he receive another gift in her place. Achilles offers him generous compensation from the future booty of the sack of Troy, but Agamemnon refuses. He wants compensation in kind—a woman for a woman, an affront for an affront. In exchange for the girl he must return to her father, he demands Achilles' prize, the fair Briseis. This is not only an act of injustice—since Achilles has done nothing that justifies punishment—it is also a grave insult to the son of Peleus. Agamemnon does not care:

> You *are* nothing to me—you and your overweening anger!
> But let this be my warning on your way:
> Since Apollo insists on taking my Chryseis,
> I'll send her back in my own ships with *my* crew,
> But I, I will be there in person at your tents
> To take Briseis in all her beauty, your own prize—
> So you can learn just how much greater I am than you
> And the next man up may shrink from matching words
>   with me,
> From hoping to rival Agamemnon strength for strength![4]

Now Achilles' own anger flares up, a mighty wrath of divine proportions, bearing death and destruction. Achilles seems to hesitate over the appropriate reaction to this affront, but his hand has already made the decision his mind has not. Agamemnon has insulted him *in public*. He has made a fellow warrior lose face. This insult, this sullying of his person (the word *persona* means the mask an actor wears on stage), can be erased only with blood:

> Anguish gripped Achilles.
> The heart in his rugged chest was pounding, torn . . .
> Should he draw the long sharp sword slung at his hip,
> Thrust through the ranks and kill Agamemnon now?—
> Or check his rage and beat his fury down?
> As his racing spirit veered back and forth,
> Just as he drew his huge blade from its sheath,
> Down from the vaulting heavens swept Athena,
> The white-armed goddess Hera sped her down:
> Hera loved both men and cared for both alike.
> Rearing behind him Pallas seized his fiery hair—
> Only Achilles saw her, none of the other fighters—
> Struck with wonder he spun around, he knew her at once,
> Pallas Athena! The terrible blazing of those eyes,
> And his winged words went flying.[5]

Achilles obeys Athena, who commands him to sheath his sword—but his anger is not calmed. It would perhaps have been better to let Achilles assuage his anger immediately. When the goddess of reason attempts to restrain it, she only stirs it up. As time passes, his murderous anger grows, his bloodlust deepens. Anger that is not released immediately will explode later with ten times the force, hurling down to the House of Death the souls of many great fighters. As a man of honor, Achilles does not conceal what is in his heart. "Anger," writes Aristotle in the *Rhetoric*, "may be defined as a desire, accompanied by pain, for a conspicuous revenge for a conspicuous slight at the hands of men who have no call to slight oneself or one's friends."[6] Peleus' son has been slighted. He answers King Agamemnon with harsh words, a first installment—"emotional first aid," if you will, for the pain that tears at his breast. The real cure will come later. After the insults, he turns to threats:

> Staggering drunk with your dog's eyes, your fawn's heart!
> Never once did you arm with the troops and go to battle
> or risk an ambush packed with Achaea's picked men—
> you lack the courage, you can see death coming . . .
> I tell you this and I swear a mighty oath upon it . . .
> Someday, I swear, a yearning for Achilles will strike
> Achaea's sons and all your armies! But then, Atrides,
> Harrowed as you will be, *nothing* you can do can save
>   you—
> Not when your hordes of fighters drop and die,
> Cut down by the hands of man-killing Hector! Then—
> Then, you will tear your heart out, desperate, raging
> That you disgraced the best of the Achaeans.[7]

Someone must pay for the affront suffered by the "best of the Achaeans." In the end, many will, including Achilles himself. Note that the political issues (What is the war about? Who will win it?) are of little significance for Achilles, or for his great rival, Hector. In the world of the Greek heroes, everything is personal, even politics—perhaps especially politics.

Anger is omnipresent. Repressed or expressed, it is an unavoidable component of our existence. The "fight or flight" reaction to stress hormones evolved over thousands of years as a basic survival mechanism.[8] It is an algorithm that is written within the very first drafts of our mental programming. When we identify a threat, the brain and nervous system provoke an accelerated secretion of adrenaline and order the adrenal glands to start producing cortisol. The heart rate increases; breathing becomes more rapid, providing the body with extra oxygen; the pupils dilate; blood vessels in less important areas (like the stomach and skin) constrict, and blood is directed to muscles in the limbs. Emergency reserves of glucose are released. We are in a state of extreme physical agitation and extreme readiness for action: fight or flight. The body is now geared for immediate action. If you have chosen flight, adrenaline will help you run away from the threat; if you have chosen attack, it is mixed with other chemical secretions that make us move in the opposite direction, toward the adversary. Anger impels us forward; it chases away fear (and sometimes reason), and allows us to bear stronger pain than we would have been able to endure otherwise, before the heart overflowed with rage.[9]

What is it that pushes us to choose one thing rather than another? Our reaction depends to a certain extent on biological mechanisms (some reflexes do not pass through the brain at all). But our choice also depends on the education we have received and on the culture in which we live.[10] In other words, Achilles' physiological reaction, faced with what he perceives as a threat against his person, is universal—a murderous cocktail of adrenaline, cortisol, and testosterone. But *what*, exactly, the son of Peleus considers a personal threat, and what others perceive as a legitimate reaction to such a threat, can change radically from culture to culture.[11] At what point do the words and actions of another person become an existential threat, even if they constitute no physical danger whatsoever? How much violence should be used to remove this threat? The answers that cultures give to these questions establish the limits of anger as a social phenomenon. Beyond those limits, one is no longer rational but a coward or a madman, rather than a hero whose rage deserves to be praised in song. Cultures mark the moment when biochemistry and ethos part ways, when a man moves from having "lost his patience" to having "lost his head" to having "lost his mind."

Achilles is mad. He is not crazy; his anger is socially legitimate. It is not awful, but awesome. This chapter focuses on angry men—more specifically, on men whose anger is seen by their culture as "manly."

Such anger is "un-Christian." Christ Himself often spoke and acted like an angry man, expressing rage toward the Pharisees, toward the money changers in the Temple, even toward the barren fig tree. What Christ *never* did was lose His temper in response to attacks on His manly honor. He bears slights and affronts without comment, and commands His disciples to do the same—to turn the other cheek. He dies on the Cross forgiving his enemies and detractors. This, for macho cultures, is deeply shameful, especially for a person who has the *power* to exact revenge. In a momentous decision, the Church, from its earliest days, forbade its members to bear arms (although, with time, it allowed exceptions to this rule in the form of the military orders). In a world soon to be dominated by Germanic warlords and their angry retainers, this made the Church exceptionally vulnerable. Men of the cloth were feminine in a culture that despised women and "girly men." They were unarmed in a society that worshiped the sword. Anger was the warrior's mortal sin; for noncombatants, it was a mortal threat.

Of course, there were other types of anger that did threaten the souls of ecclesiastics—repressed anger that remained pent up.

> [Such people, writes John Cassian,] maintain a rancorous spirit against those with whom they are upset, and although they deny orally that they are angry, they manifest the deepest anger by their actions. They neither approach them with an appropriate word nor speak to them with ordinary civility, and in this regard they do not consider themselves in the wrong, because they do not demand vengeance for their annoyance. Yet because they do not dare to or cannot bring it out into the open, they turn the poison of their wrath back to their own destruction, brooding over it in their hearts and in glum silence digesting it within themselves.[12]

In warrior cultures, only unmanly men are afraid or unable to bring their anger out into the open. Anger does not constitute a weakness or a character flaw. It is certainly not a mortal sin. On the contrary, it is an essential constituent of the warrior's personality. The warrior's capacity to mobilize physical and moral resources to risk his own life and limb, and the lives of others, is a vital asset, a praiseworthy virtue. In warrior societies, natural selection privileges those males capable of effectively using anger to dispose of their own and the community's enemies. In peaceful, orderly societies, these same character traits are denounced as "antisocial," and self-restraint is extolled. Aggression is frowned on, anger deplored. The person with a "short fuse" is dangerous; violence is never considered the right course. Think of the Jewish community in the Diaspora. Centuries ago, the Jew lost his right to use violence in the often hostile world of non-Jews. He had to learn to swallow his pride and avoid at all costs an explosion that could lead to attack and might have catastrophic results for the entire Jewish community.[13] A Jew was culturally programmed to prefer flight, unless there was no other way. In a *shtetl* (Jewish village in eastern Europe), a Jewish Achilles would have meant no end of trouble.

But Achilles did not live in a little Jewish village in the Diaspora; he lived in ancient Greece, in the Heroic Age. In warrior societies, one does not seek alternatives to violence. Violence saves time; violence sends the clearest messages; violence is the universal language of men.

Violence, then, is a way of life in many societies. Anger in such societies is both feared and praised. But the raging Achilles has a heel. In Greek society, as in any warrior society, members of the caste of combatants suffer from a frightening dissonance between their abnormal insensitivity to physical danger and their hypersensitivity to anything that threatens their status. "Heroes" are expected to react with almost suicidal indifference to threats against their life and bodily integrity. They are expected to fight when common opinion (and common sense) would choose flight. They are expected to take no account of physical pain, terrible injuries, even certain death. The fighter despises death; his honor is dearer to him than his life. But at the same time, combatants react with terrible explosions of anger and violence to relatively minor attacks on their honor, almost invisible slights that others would bear without pain or shame. An ill-chosen word, a salutation expressing a real or imaginary lack of respect, a minuscule affront (always in the eyes of the beholder) causes blue blood to boil, inflicts deep wounds on the fighter's sensitive soul, spiritual wounds that only wounds of flesh and blood will cure. In warrior societies, the fighter who has lost face has lost the taste for life. He becomes a nonperson, a dishonored man. A samurai who disgraces himself by surrendering will gladly collaborate with his captors, since he is socially dead in his own society. A macho man who allows his honor to be compromised is symbolically emasculated. He becomes a woman, a laughingstock, a legitimate prey for real men.

The affronts are not important in themselves. They are an expression of the fact that the offenders do not fear the reaction of the offended, that they do not respect him. The explosion of anger is not an overreaction to some minor grievance, but an attempt to protect the moral integrity and the social status of someone whose very existence has been called into question by the offense. Like the princess whose skin was so sensitive that dozens of mattresses could not protect her from being bruised by a tiny pea, the warrior is endowed with skin so sensitive that each attack may prove fatal for the offender or the offended—often for both.

We may find all this irrational, but in societies where status plays a central role, anger is considered a justified, if hasty, response to a threat to one's status. It's surprising to find that Aristotle, the great believer in temperance, is not unsympathetic to the angry:

> Let us then observe the fact that lack of self-control with regard to temper [*thoumos*, anger] is also less shameful than the form relating to appetites. For one's temper in such cases seems to hear what reason says, but to mishear it. . . .

For reason, or sensory appearances, indicate "unprovoked aggression" or "insult," and temper, as if having reasoned it out that this sort of thing is cause for going to war [or attacking], moves into angry mode at once; whereas appetite only needs reason or perception to say "pleasant" for it to rush off to enjoy it. So temper follows reason, in a way, but appetite does not. In that case, not being able to control it [appetite] is the more shameful, in so far as the person behaving uncontrollably in regard to temper is in a way giving in to reason.[14]

The angry man recognizes a real threat and gives in to *reason*. The only problem is that instead of avenging himself reasonably (as he should), the angry man acts rashly.

Acting rashly in obedience to the dictates of one's offended ego is characteristic of the heroes of feudal-era epics *(chansons de geste)*. The most famous of these epic poems, *La Chanson de Roland* (The Song of Roland), probably composed in the eleventh century, focuses on anger and its consequences. But as we shall see, the song also expresses certain unheroic doubts.[15] Roland—the nephew of Charlemagne, king of the Franks and emperor of the Romans—and Ganelon, Roland's stepfather, participate in a council summoned by the emperor. They are discussing a Muslim proposal for a peace agreement. After many defeats on the battlefield, the Muslims say they are willing to convert to Christianity and become Charlemagne's vassals on condition that the Christian troops withdraw from conquered Spain. They offer the Christians many gifts. Roland, who represents the faction favoring war, urges rejection of the Muslim proposal; Ganelon advocates accepting it and ending the war. Ganelon's recommendation carries the day, and Roland suggests that his stepfather be sent to lead the negotiations with the Muslims. The mission is delicate, for any negotiation dealing with affairs of honor proves to be extremely dangerous and often deadly for the messengers. Their first emissaries to the Muslims were executed. Ganelon does not accept his assignment in good spirit.

Count Ganelon began to choke,
pulls from his neck the great furs of marten
and stands there now, in his silken tunic,
eyes full of lights, the look on him of fury,
he has the body, the great chest of a lord;
stood there so fair, all his peers gazed on him;
said to Roland: "Madman, what makes you rave?
Every man knows I am your stepfather,
Yet you named me to go to Marsilion.
Now if God grants that I come back from there,
You will have trouble. I'll start a feud with you,
it will go on till the end of your life."
Roland replies: "What wild words—all that blustering!
    Every man knows that
threats don't worry me. But we need a wise man to bring
    the message:
If the king wills, I'll gladly go in your place."

Ganelon answers: "You will not go for me,
You're not my man, and I am not your lord.
Charles commands me to perform this service:
I'll go to Marsilion in Saragossa.
And I tell you, I'll play a few wild tricks
Before I cool the anger in me now."
When he heard that, Roland began to laugh.
Ganelon sees: Roland laughing at him!
and feels such pain he almost bursts with rage,
needs little more to go out of his mind;

says to the Count: "I have no love for you,
you *made* this choice fall on me, and that was wrong.
Just Emperor, here I am, before you.
I have one will: to fulfill your command."[16]

Ganelon is not a coward. He has already proven his valor in many battles. What provokes this explosion of anger is not the danger of the mission, but the fact that Roland does not show the respect expected from a son, even a stepson. A son does not name his father to head a dangerous mission, unless he is sure that Ganelon wants it. The author of *The Song of Roland* has no love for Ganelon. The latter is the bad guy, the *felon,* of the story. His "wild trick" consists in persuading the Muslims to ambush the Frankish rearguard, which is under Roland's command. The Muslims, a thousand times more numerous than the Franks, will succeed in massacring the twenty thousand Christians. Yet the poet cannot hide his admiration for Ganelon when the traitor is giving free rein to his anger. As the fury boils up within him, Ganelon becomes beautiful: "eyes full of lights, the look on him of fury, / he has the body, the great chest of a lord; / stood there so fair, all his peers gazed on him."

Note the escalation in the exchange of insults between the protagonists. After the first affront inflicted on his stepfather, Roland aggravates the situation: he volunteers to replace Ganelon, thus implying that the latter is afraid of going. Ganelon reacts in the only way he can to save his honor: he insists on accomplishing the mission, while publicly threatening that Roland will pay dearly for his arrogance. This is the official challenge, the equivalent of what would later become "throwing down the gauntlet." This public threat in response to an attack on one's honor transforms a street brawl into a duel—a ceremonial act that follows strict rules. It is an execution, not an assassination. Yet despite the threats and the harsh language (Ganelon calls his stepson a rogue, a fool, and a madman), the point of no return between Roland and Ganelon is reached only at the moment when Roland starts to laugh. Of course, an "official" confrontation has been decreed, but an appropriate intervention could still smooth out the difficulties. Warrior assemblies are not debating clubs; they are meetings where threats and curses are constantly being exchanged and violence is never far from the surface. Threats and rough language between "worthy" opponents do not cause irreparable damage to their status-sensitive skins—but laughter does. As soon as Roland laughs at his stepfather in full view of his companions, reconciliation ceases to be possible. Laughter is the ultimate expression of symbolic violence, much worse than physical attack. If you do not take your opponent seriously, it means that he is already dead (as a man) in your eyes. It is thus scarcely surprising that Ganelon almost loses his head and that his language, generally rich (he is the most complex and intelligent of the Frankish nobles), unconsciously slides into the most primary vocabulary of human beings: "I have no love for you!"

Ganelon's plot succeeds. The Muslims ambush the Frankish rearguard at Roncevaux. Roland refuses to blow his horn, the Oliphant, to summon help; and after a heroic battle, every man in his force is slain. Only then does Roland blow the Oliphant, to let the emperor and his men know that the deed is done. He arranges the bodies of his fallen comrades to face the enemy—lest anyone accuse even one of them of fleeing the battle scene—and dies after delivering a long farewell speech to his beloved sword, Durendal. The returning Franks then defeat the Muslim forces and exact a heavy price for their treachery. What seems astonishing—at least to the modern reader—is that for the peers of Roland and Ganelon, the annihilation of the Frankish rearguard is a regrettable consequence of a perhaps rash, but not unjustifiable, action. Like Aristotle, they can see the logic of anger, though they regret its haste. In the course of the traitor's trial, after Charlemagne's victory, Ganelon fiercely denies any accusation of felony:

I was in that army with the emperor
and served him well, in love and loyalty.
Then his nephew Roland began to hate me,
And he doomed me to die an outrageous death:
I was sent as messenger to King Marsilion.
I used my wits, and I came back alive.
Now I had challenged Roland, that great fighter,
And Oliver, and all of their companions:
King Charles heard it, and all his noble barons.
I took *revenge*, but there's no treason there.[17]

The barons accept these arguments and propose that the emperor release Ganelon. Certainly the many deaths are lamentable, but the execution of Ganelon will not bring the dead back. Ganelon has done what any self-respecting man would do if his honor were offended. His thirst for vengeance being now satisfied, there is no reason to think that he will not henceforth serve the emperor faithfully. Charlemagne is unconvinced (not because he refutes this argument, but because the desire for vengeance burns in *his* veins), but he remains powerless in the face of the barons' verdict. Only direct divine intervention (through the intermediary of a legal duel imposed by Thierry, the brother of Lord Geoffrey, one of the emperor's men) assures a death sentence for Ganelon.

It seems that the problem with Ganelon's behavior is not the death of so many innocent bystanders. In a world ruled by anger and honor, bystanders always pay the price. It is certainly not the traitor's indifference to the political consequences of his treason; Roland is as indifferent to his mission as his stepfather. The weak point in Ganelon's defense is that he plotted. He did not let his boiling blood take over, but held back. He did not lose his head; he was calculating.

Calculation is not worthy of a hero. Yes, Odysseus is cunning and calculating, but he is not a heroes' hero. Heroes' heroes, men like Achilles and Hector, are not as obsessed with saving their lives or with going home to their wives as the king of Ithaca. They die heroically in the battlefield. Roland is such a hero. "Roland is valiant," the author notes, "Oliver is wise." A real hero should not be too smart, or wage war by stratagems; he charges straight at the enemy—like an honorable man.

But the *Song of Roland*—composed in an era when the merchant class, with its cost-benefit rationality, was on the ascent—is not immune to the changes that were occurring in society. Merchants thought that uncontrolled violence was bad for business. They hated disorder, and they particularly hated waste. Whatever their differences, Ganelon and Roland were part of a joint enterprise. Getting the job done was always supposed to come first. They should not have solved their personal problems at the company's expense. Rather unexpectedly, Roland's valiant friend Oliver questions the sacred irrationality of the angry, honor-possessed warrior: "Companion, it is your doing. / I will tell you what makes a vassal good: / it is judgment, it is never madness; / restraint is worth more than the raw nerve of a fool. / Frenchmen are dead because of your wildness."[18] But that is only one moment of rationality, one levelheaded note against a chorus of angry voices—whose worst fear is that even after they die, they will be put to shame. They die so that "no one sings a bad song of their swords."[19]

In this turbulent sea of boiling emotion, Ganelon has acted in cold blood. He could have acted immediately when Roland laughed at him. He chose to wait. He made plans. He protected himself from danger and acted through the agency of someone else. "The more plotting people do," notes Aristotle, "the more unjust they are. Now, the person who tends to lose his temper does not plot, and neither does temper [anger], but is open."[20] Plotting is unjust. A truly angry man does not plot or plan; he acts. This is why Othello is tragic and Iago despicable.

Premeditation ("plotting") implies responsibility; losing your temper relieves you of it. We still believe this. When rage surges up from the depths of our souls, the dams of culture and reason crumble.

ANGER

Anger—volcanic, uncalculating, unplotting anger—is "irrepressible."
But is it really? Or, more importantly, is our reaction to it as neutral as
the flood metaphor implies? A look at the decisions handed down by
courts through the ages tells a different story. Anger turns out to be
closely correlated with class and gender. For physical violence as for
sexual aggression, the "unbearability" of the provocation is often defined after the fact. First, there is the explosion of violence, and then, if
the aggressor is socially worthy of defense, a suitable provocation is
found. If courts think that gay politicians like Harvey Milk are a nui-
sance, they will be willing to accept even a Twinkie defense.[21] If they
think that disgracing "the best of the Achaeans" is unpardonable, they
will not imprison Achilles, but sing his praises. The definition of an act
as "unbearable provocation" is to a great extent the expression of a social norm, not a quality that is internal or inherent in the act itself. In
other words, the moment you cease to be responsible is not determined
by "hard facts" (the levels of hormones in your blood, or a carefully defined scale of provocations), but by a culture's gut reaction to the responsibility triangle: the act (is it socially acceptable?), the aggressor
(can we feel empathy for the person?), and the victim (how similar is
the individual to "us"?). Like Abraham Lincoln's famous book review
("people who like this sort of thing will find this the sort of thing they
like"), irrepressible urges are justifiable only to those who want to jus-
tify them. Not all powerful appetites have such dedicated defenders. A
man cannot maintain that the possessions of somebody else aroused in
him an irrepressible envy or an insurmountable cupidity. He would
have a hard time persuading a court that his gluttony impelled him
against his will to swoop down upon a filet mignon in a restaurant. The
possessions of the powerful always remain more sacred than the bodies
of the weak.

Gradually, however, a change occurred in the social position of
anger. The Western world is no longer ruled by its Rolands and Ga-
nelons. It is ruled by its businessmen. The merchants, usurers, and

moneylenders colluded with the kings and the clergy to curb Rolandian wrath. They mocked it in endless spoofs, warned against it in sermons and morality tales, promised its advocates everlasting damnation, and passed laws that exacted a heavy price for personal vendettas. They cited philosophers throughout the ages who castigated the evils of wildness (warriors do not write philosophy; philosophers do not defend unreason). Private wars were outlawed by the state, and finally even the last relic of honor-related violence, the duel, was banned. The European bourgeoisie domesticated its warrior class. And while men in three-piece suits are just as capable of violence as their sword-wielding predecessors, they are much less sympathetic to unrestrained (wasteful) outbursts and much more prone to plotting (well-planned warfare). In the West today, lack of restraint is definitely low-class. Empathy for the aggressor now tends to travel on a vertical plane (he is a primitive person whose lack of education made him a victim of his basic urges) rather than on a horizontal plane (he is like me; I would have done the same thing).

This holds true for the West's attitude toward non-Western cultures. The anger of formerly colonized and formerly enslaved people is seen as an irrational force. They make a fuss about unimportant things (honor, religion, tradition). They use the once-universal language of violence to communicate with people who speak a different dialect. What really matters for Westerners is hard facts, hard cash, hard disks. We cannot really respect our angry, irrational (childish) neighbors. They must first earn our respect by becoming more like us. In this dialogue, both parties persistently misunderstand each other's messages, mutually imputing insensitivity and ill-will. Both insist that arguments no longer work. They attack us in violent outbursts of righteous anger, because by our unthinking superior attitude (unthinking because for us self-evident) we offend not only their faith and their values, but their very identity as men (we are talking about men) worthy of respect. We prefer to concentrate on the rage (totally unacceptable, according to our new standards) and ignore the motivations. We use their rage to release *us* from responsibility. Both sides feel that they have been left no choice. They're trying to teach us a lesson we fail to understand. We defend ourselves with great violence (though without ever losing our self-control) against their murderous rage and their angry God.

But not so long ago, rage was good enough for our own God. The anger of Jehovah is kindled when the members of His chosen people worship other gods. But He has other reasons to be angry. In the course of their peregrinations in the Sinai Desert, the Israelites often got on the Lord's nerves: "Now the people complained about their hardships in the hearing of the Lord, and when he heard them his anger was aroused. The fire from the Lord burned among them and consumed some of the outskirts of the camp."[22] Later, when the Israelites complained of the food provided to them by the Lord and Moses in the desert, "the Lord became exceedingly angry."[23] In chapter 23 of the Book of Numbers, God supplies quail to the Israelites, but their table manners mortify Him: "While the meat was still between their teeth, and before it could be consumed, the anger of the Lord burned against the people, and the Lord struck them with a severe plague."[24] In the following chapter, Aaron and Miriam criticize Moses for having married an Ethiopian woman: "The anger of the Lord turned against them and he left them."[25] This time, He is content with striking Miriam with leprosy (Aaron gets out safely, as he did in the episode of the Golden Calf). After the episode of twelve explorers sent to the Promised Land (they have the bad idea of reporting the truth, rather than the idyllic version that God wanted to hear), God, seized with a truly murderous rage, wants to annihilate all of the tribes of Israel and create in their place a new people. What saves the people from destruction is the fact that God's fear of what people might say is even greater than His anger. Moses manages to dissuade the angry Jehovah by declaring: "If you put these people to death all at one time, the nations who have heard this report about you will say, 'The Lord was not able to bring these people into the land he promised them on oath, so he slaughtered them in the desert.'"[26] The fear of being made the subject of a "bad song" is common to both Roland and the God of Israel.

God allows Himself to lose His temper and to act violently, because nobody can criticize Him. Critics have always been unpopular—but if we criticize the Almighty, we may be risking our lives. What can we do? Well, we have to praise Him, venerate Him, glorify Him, exalt Him, so that He will calm down and take pity on us. It is important to stress that we are totally unworthy of the Master's attention, and still less of His fury. We have sinned, betrayed, and gone astray. Forgive us; forgiving is divine. If the Lord still feels a propensity to violence, why not aim it at more suitable objects? It is always good to tell Him about the terrible misdeeds of the idolatrous and the awful things they say about Him and His chosen people. It is important to tell Him that they mock His force and are not impressed by His anger: "Pour out your wrath on the nations that do not acknowledge you, on the kingdoms that do not call on your name; for they have devoured Jacob and destroyed his homeland. . . . Why should the nations say, 'Where is their God?' Before our eyes, make known among the nations that you avenge the outpoured blood of your servants."[27] And if you were thinking that the *Christian* divinity is a God of love, think again. Certainly, Christians distinguish between the God of the Old Testament—vengeful, vindictive, irritable—and the God of the New Testament, the gentle and forgiving God of love. But all this forgiving and empathy for His enemies has, it seems, left God with great resentment. Best to avoid meeting him on the Day of Wrath *(dies irae)*, when the world will be ravaged by flames and when "even the Just will be barely safe" *(cum vix justus sit securus)*. If you asked generations of fire-and-brimstone preachers, they would tell you that since His time on the Cross, when He pardoned his enemies, the Christian God has become much less clement and tends to indulge in outbursts of fury not unworthy of the God of the Old Testament.

Theologians did not quite know how to explain away God's anger. Not that humans' actions wouldn't make a man lose his temper! Quite the contrary—human beings do things that would make any man explode. The problem lies in the absence of control. A man might lose his temper—but God? Unlike mortals, God never loses control of Himself. He is always in a state of total control and divine serenity. And what about all those biblical verses stating the contrary? "Since these things," writes John Cassian, "cannot without horrible sacrilege be literally understood of him who is declared by Holy Scripture to be invisible, ineffable, incomprehensible, inestimable, simple and uncomposite, the disturbance of anger (not to mention wrath) cannot be attributed to that immutable nature without monstrous blasphemy."[28] All the verses attributing anger, wrath, and rage to God should be interpreted as metaphors. Divine fury is merely another name for divine justice. God punishes evildoers and idolaters justly and serenely.

This is a beautiful interpretation. One can formulate things more simply: if you have a "short fuse," you'd better be omnipotent. Then you'll have defenders who will find excellent explanations for each and every one of your acts. If you're not omnipotent, calm down please.

PRIDE
Superbia

Pride, the theologians tell us, is the mother of all the vices, their *fons et origo*, source and origin. It is not the last of the seven deadly sins, but the first in importance. Why is self-esteem so sinful? Because in monotheistic systems of thought, all esteem, all praise, all love belong rightfully to God alone. He is the sole wellspring of good in the world. When a rich young man addresses Jesus as "good teacher," Jesus answers curtly: "Why do you call me good? No one is good but one, that is God."[1] All creatures' good is derivative. If you examine it with the appropriate spirit of humility, you can easily trace it back to its divine source. Taking pride in human achievement, therefore, is not simply an error of logic (confusing cause and effect). It gives rise to a harmful habit in earthly beings: their habit of esteeming, loving, praising, indeed worshiping *themselves* instead of God. In the deepest sense, pride is a particularly noxious form of idolatry. The true origin of all good is forgotten, or else mentioned in passing as a remote, almost insignificant "first cause."

In all authoritarian systems, the subjects' greatest virtue is humility. The art of imperial rule, as Virgil says in the *Aeneid,* consists of sparing those who submit to Roman rule and vanquishing the proud.[2] The proud, it is implied, are by their very pride rebellious. The gods, as rulers of the universe, want their subjects to be humble and obedient. Since human pride leads to insubordination, the gods punish the proud. The One True God shares his rivals' aversion to disobedience. But He does not see the issue merely in political terms. Pride, as we shall see, threatens the very foundations of God's created world and leads the soul to utter ruin. Whereas the previous chapter focused on "secular" aspects of (masculine) anger, this chapter focuses on the religious aspect of pride in monotheistic, particularly Christian, thought.

Was the world ever free of pride? There's strong reason to doubt it. The evil inclination toward *amour propre* arose within rational creatures almost as soon as they came into being. In the Christian tradition, the angels were the first things God created. They were the "heavens" mentioned in the opening verse of Genesis, the first (immaterial) light that God's Word brought into existence. The angels—pure spirit unburdened by matter, formidably powerful, immortal—resembled God as much as any imperfect creature can resemble perfection. No labor was imposed upon them, not even the task of tending Paradise, as Adam and Eve were obliged to do. The angels knew the greatest possible happiness, the *only* true happiness: proximity to God and direct experience of His goodness. God did not hide His face from them, nor did they see their Creator as through a veil darkly. They did not have to earn this boon. It was given to them freely, from the beginning. Their one duty was to thank God, not because they were ordered to do so but because "it is good to thank the Lord and sing the praises of your name, O Most High."[3] The angels were happy with God, and God was happy with His angels.

This blissful idyll did not last long. Like a lethal virus coming out of nowhere—out of the nothingness from which God created being—pride entered the minds of some of the heavenly host, the "rebel angels," ordering them to self-destruct, to rise in an impossible revolt against the Almighty. But why? What triggered the mechanism of self-destruction? Theologians have no real answer.[4] Augustine, grappling with this question in *The City of God,* suggests the possibility that the angels were not created equal: "It must follow that the good angels are themselves assured of their eternal felicity. The other angels had not that assurance, since their bliss was destined to have an end, and there was no eternity of bliss for them to be assured of. It remains that either the angels were unequal, or, if they were equal, the good angels received the certainty of eternal felicity after the ruin of the others."[5]

Augustine is inclined to accept the former view. Without the assurance of eternal felicity, the pressures toward infelicity are bound to take over. For the bishop of Hippo, pride—the sin of preferring *amor sui* (love of self) to *amor dei* (love of God)—is an autogenous force, arising within the organism itself. *Amor dei* is unnatural for earthly creatures. Without the firm hand of God (manifest in the certainty of eternal felicity) to prevent them from turning their gaze from God to themselves, rational beings *necessarily* fall. God's intervention is an act of providential violence. What is *natural* to created beings is *amor sui,* pride.

But the question of the moral responsibility of imperfect entities vis-à-vis a perfect being came later. At first, the angels' rebellion was seen in terms of domination and resistance. Great power like the power of God arouses envy. And envy, as we have seen, stems from an implied belief in our right to be as good as, or better than, the object of our envy. Overcome with envy (pride once removed), a faction of the angels revolted against God. The leader of the rebel angels was the brilliant Morning Star, Son of the Dawn (which translates as *Lucifer* in Latin).[6] As might be expected, the rise was brief and the fall long and painful. Any assault on God is pure folly; it's suicide to even *think* that a creature can be greater than Him "than which nothing greater can be conceived." A proud creature that turns away from God is, *ipso facto,* turning against itself. Like the Greek *hubris, superbia* brings about its own downfall.

In the speech that Isaiah addresses to the king of Babel, the prophet declares:

> How you have fallen from heaven,
> O morning star, son of the dawn! [Lucifer in the Latin
>   translations]
> You have been cast down to the earth,
> You who once laid low the nations!
> You said in your heart, "I will ascend to heaven;
> I will raise my throne above the stars of God:
> I will sit enthroned on the mount of assembly,
> On the utmost heights of the sacred mountain.
> I will ascend above the tops of the clouds;
> I will make myself like the Most High."
> But you are brought down, to the grave, to the depths of
>   the pit.[7]

"I will make myself like the Most High." The Fall occurs precisely at this point. The angel who can utter these words, who can conceive such an idea, has already fallen. What follows is not the Fall, but its long and merciless punishment. Those who enjoyed intimacy with God now find themselves removed from Him; those who knew only His goodness become vessels of His wrath. The angels' pride has given birth to Hell— that place, or that state of the soul, where God is manifest not as mercy but only as justice.

Wouldn't it have been better, then, if God had refrained from creating other rational beings? Probably. For it is reason that makes self-love a sin. Unlike beasts, rational creatures should have acted more wisely. But if someone as blessed with celestial gifts as Lucifer fell from Heaven, how could less perfect creatures have done better? But the biblical God was an optimist, at least in the initial stages of Creation. Perhaps, he thought, it was the near-perfection of the angels that gave them such dangerous ideas. Perhaps humbler creatures would see the absurdity of trying to make themselves like the Most High. On the sixth day, then, God created Adam and Eve. Paradise was a moral incubator. Prior to the Fall, Adam and Eve were exempt from suffering. They, too, were offered happiness (happiness is God's elusive fruit). He even gave them a taste of that power which aroused the envy of Lucifer. They were given dominion "over the fish of the sea and the birds of the air, over the livestock over all the earth, and over all the creatures that move along the ground."[8] Too much knowledge is dangerous, thought God. Knowledge begets pride; He forbade them to eat the fruit of the Tree of Knowledge. Immortality makes one careless; He forbade them the Tree of Life. He had high hopes for them. Then he waited.

He did not have to wait long. Near the beginning of Goethe's *Faust*, Mephistopheles declares that he is so moved by the suffering of human beings that he hesitates to add to their misery. In the Garden of Eden humans were happy and the Serpent had no second thoughts. But then, Adam and Eve were not assured of eternal felicity—so what could one expect? They followed the advice of the Father of Lies. Did they actually believe Satan's promises? Did they learn nothing from the fate of Lucifer? According to Augustine, Adam (he is less certain about Eve) was not a believer. He acted not out of stupidity but out of "radical evil." Adam knew that pride (for it was pride that was offered to him) was unpardonable and that the proud always suffer a terrible fate. Yet when Eve offered him the forbidden fruit, he ate. They ate because they could not resist the temptation of becoming "like God."

Original sin caused our expulsion from Paradise. Human life became nasty, brutish, and short. Eternal damnation was always just around the corner. Yet it must be admitted that humans succeeded in being like God, at least to some extent. If they could not make Creation better (how could created beings perfect the work of the divine artificer?), they could at least change it—for the worse, it is true, but at least in *their* image and likeness. The world after the Fall was profoundly different from the world that preceded it. Change and movement were everywhere. Heaven and Hell turned into very busy places. The land had to be arduously cultivated, and life became filled with wars, turbulent emotions, crimes of passion, self-sacrifice, tragic accidents, painful misunderstandings, unhappy surprises. Sin, human sin (for God was not touched by the rebel angels' suffering as deeply as He was moved by human affliction), even brought God to unite in kind with His fallen creatures and take on their flesh, to suffer torture and humiliation at their hand, and die, broken, on the Cross. Lucifer was certainly part of all this, but Adam and Eve's sinful descendants did most of the work themselves. They could be proud of themselves.

And they *are* proud. Not of the fact that the visible world has been converted from Paradise to Hell, or even of the fact that the invisible world has become derivative—waiting for human actions, then counterbalancing them with rewards and punishments—but of a thousand other things. They are proud of their existence; or rather their very existence as fallen creatures makes them guilty of pride. To be anything but what God originally *meant* us to be is sinful. To wish to continue as morally deformed and misguided, to love ourselves in our current state, is a deadly sin. If we want an antidote to pride, we must constantly remind ourselves of our nullity. Akavya, son of Mahalalel, says: "Observe three things and you will not fall into sin: Know where you came from, where you are going, and before whom you will give account and reckoning. Where did you come from? From a stinking drop of liquid. Where are you going? To a place of dust, worms, and maggots. And before whom will you give account and reckoning? Before the King of the kings of kings, the Holy One, blessed be He."[9] The Jewish prayer of *Shema* requires the Israelite to love the Lord with all his heart and with all his soul and reflect upon His Commandments "when you sit at home and when you walk along the road, when you lie down and when you get up."[10] But humans have other things on their minds when they lie down and when they get up. Instead of remembering their total worthlessness, they want to believe that their actions and existence have value. They would like to think that they are worthy not only because He made them and uses them in His cosmic plan, but also because they—each being a specific ensemble of qualities, memories, talents, and passions—are worthy of willing and feeling.[11] They think they have the right to pursue happiness and to be happy because they are who they are, not because He is who He is. But they have no such right. They are guilty of pride.

The problem is that without pride there is no individuality—at least, not in the deep sense that one must assume vis-à-vis God. To wish to be unique, to make personal choices—even good and appropriate ones—testifies to the presence of a voice ceaselessly saying "I" when it is supposed to be saying "God."[12] For even when we call upon God to have pity on us, our "I" does not disappear. It is there, in the deceptively innocent syntax of our language and in the most basic structures of our mind. "I am human," says Terence; "I consider nothing that is human alien to me." Let's be more specific. I am I; I consider nothing that interests *me* alien to me. This tendency to make the "I" precede everything else (including God, whom the "I" worships—because it is good for him, not for Him) puts the soul in mortal danger. All sins are reruns of the original sin, the original pride. Each of our desires participates in the sin of pride, for the "I" precedes desire, motivates it, and feeds it.[13] The Buddha understood this—or so some of his more radical disciples say. The *atman,* the self, is an illusion which arouses the passions that cause suffering. One (and it is not quite clear who this "one" is) must aspire to annul it, to be liberated from desire, and to vanish in the profound eradication of all passion—a state that is called Nirvana.[14]

The great fourteenth-century German mystic Meister Eckhart sounds surprisingly "Eastern" when he speaks of divesting the self of itself as a process of liberation. One of his German sermons (preached to "nonprofessionals" and thus more daring than his Latin sermons) is dedicated to the verse, "Blessed are the poor in spirit." Eckhart explores the question: What is *true* poverty? Shedding earthly possessions is easy. To achieve blessedness, the soul must relinquish its spiritual goods. In the storm-tossed ship of the soul, everything that separates us from God is useless baggage. The soul must rid itself even of the concept of "god," since, unlike God as He is in Himself, our mental image of Him is tainted with *our* self. God is a reflection of our *amour propre*. As Eckhart says: "He is poor who does not want to fulfill the will of God, but who so lives that he is empty of his own will and the will of god as when he did not yet exist."

But Western thought, even in its most radical and daring formulations (such as Eckhart's), does not aspire to total dissolution of the self. Even when Eckhart returns to the source—to the time when he did not yet exist—the notion of individuality is still present. In fact, Eckhart's noble dream soon turns into an affirmation of the self:

> This is why I pray God to rid me of god; for my essential being is above god insofar as we consider God as the origin of creatures. Indeed, in God's own being, where God is raised above all being and all distinctions, there I was myself, there I willed myself, and I knew myself to create a man in my image. . . . Therefore also I am unborn, and from the point of view of my unborn being I shall never die. By virtue of my unborn being, I have always been, am now, and shall remain eternally. . . . In my birth all things were born, and I was the cause of myself and of all things. If I had willed it, neither I nor all other things would have come to be. And if I myself were not, god would not be either. That God is god—of this I am the cause. If I were not, God would not be god.[15]

Eckhart does not describe the depersonalized self, empty of its will as when it did not yet exist, in the humble, passive terms that we might have expected; it is not a silent reflection of the sovereign will/ being of God. Quite surprisingly, he describes the self as a co-creator. "In God's own being, where God is raised above all being and all distinctions, there *I* was myself, there *I* willed myself, and *I* knew myself to create a man in my image." But this does not satisfy Eckhart. He comes out with an even more startling claim: he has created God in *his* image. "That God is 'god'—of this I am the cause. If I were not, God would not be god." Now, the "I" speaking here is the primeval "I" and not "Meister Eckhart," but the choice of language is telling. The old temptation rears its head again.

It is not easy to rid ourselves of God. It is even harder to rid ourselves of the self. We're stuck with it, stuck with ourselves. You do not have to be a medieval theologian to be aware of the paradoxical nature of the struggle. You could be one of the fathers of modernism. In the *Octavo Notebooks*, Franz Kafka offers his own interpretation of the Tree of Knowledge and its fruit: "'If you eat it you will die' means: knowledge of Good and Evil is both a step leading to eternal life and an obstacle in the way. If you want to attain eternal life after having gained knowledge—and you will not be able to do otherwise than want it, for knowledge of good and evil *is* this will—you will have to destroy yourself, the obstacle, in order to build the step, which is the destruction."[16]

We would have been guilty of pride even if we'd chosen *not* to eat the forbidden fruit. For when we were granted the right to choose, we had already eaten from the Tree of Knowledge. What followed was the poisoned fruit of that poisoned tree. Now the only way out is to choose to act not because it is *our* will, but because it is His. This we cannot do, unless God replaces our will with His. He has done this for the good angels, and the blessed in Heaven enjoy this privilege too. Liberated at last from their freedom, they do not sin, because they *cannot sin (non posse peccare)*. But are those will-less creatures still human? When we have destroyed Pride, the mother of sin and her sinful daughters, do we continue to be ourselves?

In retrospect, it seems that God understood the absurdity of the human condition and regretted creating man. In the Book of Genesis, it is stated explicitly: "The Lord saw how great man's wickedness on the earth had become, and that every inclination of the thoughts of his heart was nothing but evil all day long. And the Lord regretted that he had made man on the earth, and his heart was filled with sadness."[17]

It isn't often that the Bible attributes sadness to God. Like remorse, it seems a thoroughly human emotion. It accompanies recognition of one's limitations—a sudden, unique flash of self-awareness. Instead of ushering in a new beginning, the Flood ends with the sad realization that what was will be. Noah has just come out of the Ark; the world is fresh and dewy, as on the sixth day of Creation; the stench of rotting corpses has not yet filled the air. On the contrary, a "pleasing aroma" is rising from the altar built by the Lord's favorite.[18] Noah has not yet gotten drunk; Ham has not yet seen his father's nakedness; men have not yet taken it into their heads to build a great city "with a tower that reaches to heaven."[19] But even at this hopeful moment of renewal, God knows that things will go badly again—that they will surely not be "very good." And God "said in his heart: 'Never again will I curse the ground because of man, for the inclination of man's heart is evil from his childhood.'"[20] But God also knows His own inclination to outbursts of lethal anger. He needs a sign, a personal reminder in the form of the rainbow, a reminder never again to annihilate "all life."[21] Since then, He has learned to restrain himself, grumbling, conspiring, waiting for the End of Days, when human pride will finally come to an end. "See, the day of the Lord is coming—a cruel day with wrath and fierce anger—to make the land desolate and destroy the sinner within it. The stars of heaven and their constellations will not show their light. The rising sun will be darkened and the moon will not give its light. I will punish the world for its evil, the wicked for their sins. I will put an end to the arrogance of the haughty and will humble the pride of the ruthless."[22] After the Day of Judgment, human choice between good and evil will disappear and sinners will be wiped off the face of the earth. No more desires, no more choices—only the will of the Lord. Then, at last, arrogance shall disappear and haughtiness come to an end.

God detests human pride.[23] But in the eyes of men, is pride such a terrible sin? I don't think so. For most people, the pride of an individual in his or her capacities, qualities, and successes is (though sometimes tedious) quite legitimate. We are proud of our achievements, of our children, of our identity. We want others to be proud of us. For the Greek hero, everlasting fame is the only reward that is worth living and dying for. We, too, want to enter our profession's Hall of Fame, or, barring that, have our fifteen seconds in the limelight. And why not be proud of our abilities? If you're Leonardo da Vinci, there's nothing wrong with saying that you are an excellent architect, engineer, inventor, designer, and painter. Of course, he's proud! Why shouldn't he be? It's true that very few of us are as gifted as Leonardo. But in our own modest way, we have reason to be proud. Even our modesty can be a source of well-deserved pride. The Talmud tells of a discussion between the sages on the question of whether true modesty still existed after the death of the virtuous Rabbi Yehuda Hanassi. "Of course it does!" said an outraged Rabbi Yossef. "I'm still around!"[24] Like Leonardo, Rabbi Yossef was merely stating a fact. It so happened he was a very modest man. Future generations needed to know that modesty had not vanished with the death of Rabbi Yehuda. Rabbi Yossef simply wanted to make sure they'd be aware of this.

For all his self-proclaimed modesty, Rabbi Yossef was part of a powerful elite: the so-called sages. Elites are proud by definition, proud even of their modesty. The pride of the powerful, moreover, is often stated as fact. The sages *are* wiser than *hoi polloi* (*am haaretz,* in Hebrew); men *are* more rational than women; masters *are* more capable of ruling than underlings. These are empirical observations, aren't they? The answer depends on the person being asked.

If you had asked me during my first year at university, I would have told you that the pride and arrogance of my professors were totally unjustified (arrogance is pride thrown in the face of others). There was something intolerable about the professors' attitude toward their students—more specifically, toward me. "Education," the Columbia philosopher Irwin Edman once said, "is the process of casting false pearls before real swine." I was in total agreement, at least with the first part of the quote. I wanted the right to question the status quo. Who gave professors the keys to academic heaven (to bind and to loose, to fail and to pass), and by what right? Why did they address me by my first name, whereas I had to address them by their academic title? Who decided that their opinion counted more in class than mine? Why did they get to say who spoke and who didn't? Who said their interpretation of Plato was better than mine? There were fairly reasonable answers to these questions, but all I could see was unwarranted power. In a thousand ways, our professors signaled that they were superior to us in knowledge and intellectual ability (off-the-cuff quotations in languages unknown to us, allusions to obscure intellectuals, references to esoteric writings, all preceded by the formula "You know, of course . . ."—of course we didn't know). In their eyes, this was not pedagogic violence but innocence incarnate. They simply *were* more experienced, more knowledgeable, and more mature. That was all.

That's never all. People with institutional power and symbolic capital use them. Our professors were institutionally arrogant, even if they were personally modest. They were supposed to act superior as part of the academic game (you can't really expect teachers to earn their position from scratch in every course they teach). The university is not an ad hoc gathering of intellectuals, but an institution that uses and abuses power. Yet this doesn't explain the strong resentment I felt on campus (much stronger than the rancor I'd felt in the army—surely a more authoritarian organization than the university). Why, then, did I react this way? Perhaps because, as the son of immigrants who'd come to Tel Aviv from Beer Sheva (a provenance that city dwellers found "quaint"), I viewed the campus as enemy territory. My professors held the keys not just to academic heaven, but to the "good society" I wanted to be part of. Success meant being invited into Israelis' living rooms; failure meant being relegated to the outer darkness. Were my professors in fact the gatekeepers of the old-boys' network? Not really. Israel is a dynamic young society with extremely fluid elites. If your parents were born in Israel, you're "old family," but this advantage disappears in the second generation—immigrants' *grandchildren* are "old." As for old boys, the only institution that breeds such networks in Israel is the army. And while some of my professors did come from upper-middle-class families, others did not. One professor who I thought represented the ultimate "Mayflower" turned out to be an immigrant of rather poor background. I was too insecure to ask and too provincial to know.

These fine distinctions, however, mattered little to me at the time. I saw more arrogance than there was, and some of the aggression I resented was no doubt a projection of my own. For me, attending college was not about getting an education; it was about launching a hostile takeover. Of course, being hostile is not the best technique for winning social acceptance. But I was too proud to charm my way in. I wanted the Old Guard to accept me, whether they wanted to or not. In a way, the latter option was better. No favors necessary.

And the goal wasn't just social mobility. For me, the university was a testing ground. In Beer Sheva, I was a big fish in a little pond (at least, *I* thought I was). But was I big enough for Tel Aviv? I had to be. My intellect was the cornerstone of my identity. I prided myself on my brain; my body mattered less to me. One could accuse me of having ten thumbs, of not knowing how to manage my finances, or of being an atrocious dancer. It wouldn't have bothered me at all. But when someone criticized my intellectual abilities, I responded like Achilles or

PRIDE

Ganelon when their honor was attacked. What was being threatened was not some aspect of my personality, but my very essence.

I reacted to my distress with a mixture of ostentation and aggressiveness. When a young male wants to assert his status in a new community, he can display his feathers like a peacock or defy the dominant males. I did both. I spread my intellectual feathers to make an impression, to show that I was an "alpha" (or A) student: I flaunted my knowledge before peers and superiors; I applied myself to studying Latin, Italian, French, and German, and I used them as much as possible; I read more than necessary, wrote more than necessary, and talked much more than necessary. When all these efforts did not suffice, I bared my claws.

I remember the first class in a seminar on medieval historical thinking, with Professor Amos Funkenstein, at the beginning of my sophomore year. I had received special permission to enroll in a seminar designed for advanced students. Funkenstein had a reputation as a brilliant man with a tendency to humiliate students he did not respect. I was advised against taking his course at such an early stage. Of course, I ignored the advice. I arrived at the first session with my muscles knotted, my throat dry, and my heart pounding. Funkenstein said a few words before engaging in a short discussion with some of the older students. He was everything I had been told he was: smart, sarcastic, impatient. A surge of anger, excitement, and fear ran through me—that cocktail of adrenaline and testosterone which precedes fight-or-flight. I fought. I raised my hand, and for long minutes I explained, in the most aggressive terms I could muster, why everything that Funkenstein had said up to that point was wrong. Silence fell upon the class. Such a violent challenge could not go unanswered. The Talmud tells of an incident in which Rav Kahana dared to defy the authority of Rabbi Yohanan; with a single glance, Rabbi Yohanan killed his obstreperous student.[25] Funkenstein's gaze was perhaps not enough to kill me, but his intellectual and institutional arsenal was more than enough to humiliate me. My arguments were half-baked and seriously flawed. But even if my reasoning had been better, he could easily have crushed me with a few sarcastic remarks.

The question was: Which reflex had I sparked within him? It turned out that in addition to fight and flight, there was another possibility. Funkenstein looked amused. He answered me with exceptional politeness, and at the end of the class he asked me to stay and talk with him. His kindness was disarming. And after all, the only thing I really wanted was respect. Funkenstein offered me a job as his research assistant. I was overjoyed. I never asked him about his memory of our first encounter in that seminar. Why had he reacted that way? Was it just intellectual curiosity, or had he seen through my insecurities? Had he seen in me a younger version of himself? Had he really been amused? It's too late to ask him now.

What would I feel, and how would I act, in the same situation? I don't know. Perhaps I'm lucky—I've never had a student like me. And my students? Obviously, they *have* got a professor like me. What does this mean? Let's just say that I'll probably never win the most-modest professor prize. No doubt the deadly sin that most people associate with me is pride. And arrogance? I'd like to believe that I'm not an arrogant man. I make every effort to avoid arrogance and to refrain from using all the advantages that my status confers. But arrogance rests lightly upon the arrogant; they barely feel it. When you're at the podium, you suddenly realize that students are just oversensitive. They make mountains out of molehills. Those who have studied the Torah develop an impressive insensitivity toward the sensitivity of others.

It once happened that Rabbi Elazar, the son of Rabbi Shimon, was coming from Migdal Gedor, from the home of his teacher. He was riding on an ass and traveling along a riverbank. And he was very happy, and he was proud of himself, because he had learned much Torah. He chanced to meet a certain man, who was extremely ugly. The man said to him: "Peace be with you, rabbi," but he did not return the man's [greeting]. He said to the man: "Worthless person, how ugly you are! Are all the people of your city as ugly as you?" The man said to him: "I do not know, but go to the craftsman who made me, and say to him: 'How ugly is this vessel that you have made!'" When Rabbi Elazar understood that he had sinned, he got down from the ass and prostrated himself before the man, and said to him: "I have sinned toward you, forgive me!" The man said: "I will not forgive you until you go to the craftsman who made me and say to him: 'How ugly is this vessel that you have made!'" Rabbi Elazar traveled behind the man until they came to his city. The people of his city came out toward him, and they said to him: "Peace be with you, rabbi, rabbi, teacher, teacher!" The man said to them: "Whom do you call 'rabbi, rabbi'?" They said to him: "The man who is riding behind you." The man said to them: "If this is a rabbi, let there be few like him in Israel!"[26]

In the end, though, the man forgives him. With all due respect, Rabbi Elazar is a person of consequence, and the ugly man is not even worthy of having his name recorded. The poor are always expected to be generous.

I am now one of those who have a name, and a title. In the social class that I have successfully joined, arrogance (or pride) is the expected norm. It is attributed not only to university professors (like me) but also to Ashkenazim (like me), to liberals (like me), and to males (like me). One might go so far as to say that socially, culturally, and even politically, this sin has become our trademark. Aren't we full of good intentions? Maybe we are, but "we" seem to be particularly good at making other people feel inferior, unworthy, stupid. Humiliation, we

forget at our own peril, can be worse than physical attacks, and much
more difficult to cure. "Anyone who makes the face of another person
turn white in public [i.e., humiliates him in public] is like a man who
sheds blood."[27] I know the feeling.

Before I joined Israel's "old" intellectual elite (which I did at the
very moment it became obsolete, even bankrupt), I was one of those
who had excellent reasons to be offended. My parents—poor, unedu-
cated Holocaust survivors—experienced a large part of the Israeli *via
dolorosa* of the unimportant. They were fumigated with DDT upon arrival, lived in housing projects, labored at difficult jobs for low wages,
endured periods of unemployment, belonged to the wrong political
party. There were a thousand daily humiliations, a thousand reminders
that they were—that we were—not as good as others. I felt these slights,
even the ones that I did not suffer directly. The feeling of resentment
that filled me during adolescence was not learned at home. My parents
accepted uncomplainingly the slaps that life landed on their cheeks.
They expected little, and were not disappointed. Their arrival in Israel
did not blunt the instinct developed among Jews in two thousand years
of exile: to swallow insults and keep going. They swallowed and kept
going. They worked hard and tried to make a better life for their children. They didn't complain even when their children were taught to
turn their backs on them (for being too Old World). But *I* had a hard
time swallowing my pride. It stuck in my craw. I was angry when they
were slighted, not because I cared so much about their feelings—immigrants' children rarely care about their parents' dignity—but because
the scorn reflected on me. I was a lot angrier when the slights were
aimed directly at me. I don't know where this attitude came from. Perhaps from the strong belief instilled in me by our high-strung and
deeply egalitarian society—the belief that inequality is a scandal, that
there is no reason I shouldn't have what you have, that I deserve the
same respect you do. Yes, such feelings exist even among Ashkenazim,
liberals, and intellectuals.

PRIDE

I have now become what as a boy I dreamed of becoming. To a large extent, I'm a member of the group that exasperated me as a boy, for immigrants' children often yearn to resemble those who act superior, to be exactly like them, to be like the "enemy." I live with this very well—it's easier to be high up than down below, to be strong rather than weak, to cause hurt rather than be hurt. I would not change places with myself. Actually, I'm not sure I live with it all that well. I know I wrote the opposite two sentences ago.

10

SELF-RIGHTEOUSNESS

Then . . . Pharaoh had a dream; and behold, he stood by the Nile. And behold there came up out of the river seven cows, fine looking and fat; and they fed in the meadow. Then behold, seven other cows came up after them out of the Nile, ugly and gaunt, and stood by the other cows on the bank of the river. And the ugly and gaunt cows ate up the seven fine looking and fat cows.

—GENESIS 41:1–4 (NEW KING JAMES VERSION, TRANSLATION MODIFIED)

Here ends the list of the seven deadly sins. After our portrait of the vices—fine looking from deplorable delights and fat from forbidden foods—it would have been appropriate to summon up the virtues, theological and cardinal: ugly from discontent and gaunt from fasting. They are watching their beautiful sisters, narrowing their green eyes, salivating. At the End of Days, the seven virtues will eat up the seven vices, and the way of the righteous will finally prosper.[1] "Sinners shall vanish from the earth and the wicked shall be no more."[2] But that final moment has not yet come. Until it does, it is hard not to get bored with discussing the virtues. The force of good resides in action, not in words. Praise of morality tends to become an excuse for moralizing. Before I offer any final remarks on sinners, allow me to sling a little mud on those who are holier than us. The eighth sin in this book deals with deception—specifically, with the deceptions and self-deceptions of the righteous.

It is no accident that lying was omitted from the original list of sins. In theory, there is nothing nobler than the truth: "I am the way and the truth and the life," says Christ.[3] Truth is divine. The problem is that, for humans, telling the truth—the whole truth and nothing but the truth—is impossible. Whenever we lay our hand on the Bible and make this promise, we perjure ourselves. No matter how hard we try, we speak untruths, partial truths, quasi-truths. We can't help it.

This, however, is not the reason lying was excluded from the list. We cannot help being envious, angry, and proud; yet envy, anger, and pride are all on the list. Lying is different. It is the special transgression of shepherds—of those who are in charge of the less spiritually advanced. They do not like their vices to be the focus of attention. In this imperfect world, nontruth can render truth a great service. The whole truth can be quite shocking. Partial truth, half-truth, the occasional lie are easier to digest by the tender souls of the faithful. Truth must be handled with great care: "There is much truth to the statement that no one can be saved without being predestined and without having faith and grace," writes Ignatius of Loyola, founder of the Jesuit order. "Still, we should exercise great caution when speaking and teaching about these matters."[4] Caution is important. One must at times be jesuitical.

The moral duty to present half-truths to the uninitiated has deep roots. Elitist systems of thought presume that the majority of human beings live in a state of false consciousness. They are imprisoned in the sensual world of their flesh. Since they constantly misinterpret the world, their pleasures are false and their sorrows are false. To be liberated, humans must abandon their commonsense notions and accept the Truth: "Gnosis," the "Torah of Moses," the "Prophecy of Muhammad," the "Good Tidings" of Christ. This redemptive knowledge is not made manifest to everyone at all times. It trickles down from above through a special group of mediators—seers and visionaries who perceive the Truth and transmit it to others. The messages are often cryptic; but since they are supposed to be reflections of immutable truth, their literal meaning becomes unsatisfactory as time passes. They need interpretation. A whole class of spiritually privileged interpreters emerges to give the faithful up-to-date versions of the original message. They are continually unearthing hidden levels of meaning that were lying beneath Truth's literal surface. Thus, while Truth remains constant, its decoding is in a state of flux. Every exegete is aware of this sleight of the textual hand. But as with magic, the mechanics of deconstructing and reconstructing Truth are best kept hidden, lest they sow the seeds of doubt in the heart of simple believers. Furthermore, parts of the Truth, the *arcana fidei* (secrets of the Faith), or *Torat ha-emet* (the true, mystical meaning of the Torah), are deemed too dangerous to be fully revealed and are presented to the faithful only in diluted, bowdlerized form.

The spiritually privileged interpreters of sacred truth are superior beings. This has little to do with their personal merits and everything to do with their role as mediators. Their authority comes from their privileged access to the source or sources of true, redemptive knowledge; and the respect owed to them is an extension of the respect owed to the sacred texts or the gods. But human nature tends to blur the distinction. When you've become used to expressing your opinion as certitude, you get rather impatient not only with competing interpretations (unprofessional, dangerous, heretical), but even with heavenly voices. In a dramatic debate between Rabbi Eliezer and the other sages on a relatively minor halakhic point (when is a certain type of oven considered finished?), a divine voice from Heaven decreed that Rabbi Eliezer was right and that the law was as he said. Rabbi Yehoshua, representing the majority opinion, replied: "It [the Torah] is not in heaven!"[5] In other words, God provides the sacred text (the Torah); its interpretation is in the hands of the sages. It is better for God, who is in Heaven, not to interfere in the pious disputes of His interpreters on earth. In fact, it was later decided that heavenly voices should be ignored.

A person whose voice replaces the Lord's tends to consider himself an extension—albeit partial and imperfect—of the Lord Himself. In the Catholic tradition, the idea of the holy interpreter focused on the person of the pope, who acquired responsibility for the *magisterium,* the right to offer authoritative teaching. It all began with Jesus' cryptic words to Saint Peter: "And I also say to you that you are Peter, and on this rock I will build My church, and the gates of Hades shall not prevail against it. And I will give you the keys of the kingdom of heaven, and whatever you bind on earth will be bound in heaven, and whatever you loose on earth will be loosed in heaven."[6]

The power to bind and to loose on earth and in Heaven is great indeed. Soon it was seen as belonging not only to Peter, but to all his successors, the popes of Rome. After a while, being a successor was not enough. Shortly after his coronation in 1198, Pope Innocent III wrote: "Verily the Vicar of Christ, the successor of Peter, the anointed of the Lord, the God of Pharaoh is set midway between God and man, below God but above man, less than God but more than man, judging all other men, but himself judged by none."[7] Of course, while the pope is the symbolic embodiment of the *magisterium,* this power is delegated to the entire class of authorized exegetes and theologians.

In the Jewish community, these impressive powers were more democratically distributed among the sages. The sages, too, saw (and see) themselves as positioned midway between God and man. Loving and respecting them was a religious duty not unlike that of loving and respecting the Lord. Indeed, it could be deduced from the commandment to fear God.

Simeon the Imsonite used to expound on the word *eth* [an optional indicator of the accusative] wherever it occurred in the Torah [explaining that it always implied that something was to be added to the explicit meaning of the text]. Yet when he reached the verse "[*eth*] the Lord thy God thou shall fear" (Deuteronomy 6:13), he abstained. His pupils thereupon said to him: "Rabbi, what will now become of all the other *eths* which you have expounded on?" He replied to them: "Just as I have received my reward for interpreting every [other] *eth*, so I shall receive a reward for abstaining" [from interpreting this one]. Finally, however, Rabbi Akiva came and taught: "[*eth*] the Lord thy God thou shall fear" implies that one must also fear [or respect] the sages.[8]

Rabbi Simeon was reluctant to see in so fundamental a commandment—the fear of God—an allusion to men; for what is implicit in the text is usually more important than what is stated explicitly. God is the signified, not the signifier. How can He be the literal surface meaning from which you deduce deeper truths? But Rabbi Akiva does not share Rabbi Simeon's misgivings. For him, the fear of God and the fear of sages belong to the same category—on the textual level, in any case, and perhaps not only there. God's holy interpreters form a special category of humanity, having much in common with God Himself, whose mouthpieces they are.

As such, they allow themselves what is allowed to God: the right to act without providing explanations. *Quod licet jovi licet et his bobus*— What is permitted to Jove is permitted to these oxen. The Lord commands, "Act according to the law they teach you and the decision they give you. Do not turn aside from what they tell you, to the right or to the left."[9] How far must one avoid turning? In his exegesis on this verse from Deuteronomy, Moses Nachmanides, a thirteenth-century rabbi from Spain, offers an answer:

> Even if you are told that right is left or that left is right, says Rashi [author of a canonical twelfth-century gloss on the Bible]. This means: even if you think in your heart that they are wrong and it is as simple as telling your left from your right, act according to their commandments, and say not, "How will I eat this clearly [nonkosher] fat?" or "How will I kill this innocent person?" On the contrary, you will say: "Thus I was commanded by the Master of the commandments: that I will execute all His commandments, as those who stand before Him in a place of His choosing order me, and as according to their interpretation He gave me the Torah—even if they are wrong."[10]

The wonderful power of giving meaning to the word of God is, in the words of the great thirteenth-century canonist Hostiensis, "miraculous and against the laws of nature" (miraculosa et contra naturam). It gives the pope the power to declare that night is day, that right is wrong, and that triangles are circles.[11] This does not mean that the holy interpreters are without stain or blemish, even in their own eyes. The pope, though he is the Vicar of Christ, is a human being. If he is exempt from judgment in this world, he certainly isn't in the next. Hostiensis even notes rather sourly that the pope cannot "really" change triangles into circles. As for Jewish sages, they are famously realistic and frank about their moral failings. The Talmud is full of sages who succumb to every human vice. It even declares that greater men have a greater inclination (yetser) to sin.[12] But self-righteousness does not require that its victims believe themselves sinless. It is enough that they adopt double standards. There are good reasons for this. Holy interpreters have a duty to correct their flock. If they admit their own failures, errors, and sins, their flock will be less amenable to correction, and the admission will reflect badly on God, whose agents they are. One should therefore think twice before admitting error, as Bernard Gui wisely suggests in his *Inquisitor's Manual:*

> Moreover, the laity would be scandalized if an inquisitorial investigation of someone were abandoned without a conviction, and their faith would thereby be weakened if they saw that learned men were being ridiculed by ignorant and vile persons. For they believe us to have readily at our disposal such clear and evident arguments for the Faith, that no person could face us without us knowing immediately how to convince him in such a way that even laymen would understand our arguments. It is therefore not expedient to discuss the Faith with astute heretics in the presence of laymen.[13]

The Inquisition used extremely problematic methods—not just from a modern point of view, but from a medieval perspective as well. It trampled underfoot every basic right of the accused. Suspects were incarcerated for long periods, tortured physically and psychologically, denied legal aid, denied the right to know the charges against them, isolated, humiliated, consistently lied to. But all this did not prevent inquisitors from feeling that they themselves were victims rather than perpetrators. Gui was angry at suspected heretics for not being more open about their crimes. This would have made the inquisitor's job more straightforward. As it was, they caused great anguish for their righteous interrogators: "Under such circumstances [in which heretics refused to admit their heresy openly], serious problems beset the inquisitor from every side. On the one hand, his conscience torments him if punishment is meted out to an individual who has neither confessed nor been proved guilty; on the other hand, the inquisitor—familiar through long experience with the falsity, cunning, and malice of such persons—feels even greater anguish if by their astuteness and cunning they escape punishment, to the detriment of the faith."[14]

The righteous interrogators never change their mindset or their methods. They bend the rules in the service of a higher good (the Faith, the State, Democracy). They are forced by their victims to act in apparently immoral ways, but this is the victims' fault. It is also the fault of the public at large. The half-hearted bystanders lack understanding and are too easily scandalized. Hence, things must be concealed from their eyes. What must be concealed? All sorts of unpleasantness—ranging from interrogators' "honest" mistakes, pedophile priests, and greedy rabbis, to not-so-humanistic aspects of the Halakha.

When I was a soldier, I was required to attend a seminar on Jewish ethics. A rabbi gave us a lecture on one of the most beautiful commandments of Judaism: "You shall not stand upon the blood of your neighbor."[15] A person is not allowed to simply watch from the sidelines when his neighbor's life is in danger. "Is a non-Jew included in the term 'your neighbor'?" I asked. The rabbi's face darkened. Obviously, the question did not please him. "Why do we have to speak of this?" he retorted—and continued to lecture us on Jewish ethics. And indeed, why do we have to speak of this? Bernard Gui and Ignatius of Loyola would have agreed with the rabbi. Some issues call for great caution. There are parts of sacred truth that one should avoid discussing in the presence of non-Jews, astute heretics, and young men, so clever in their own eyes. And who was I to judge, anyway? Only those who have deep knowledge and understanding, only those who see the big picture, can judge.

Jesus, a rabbi himself, did not like double standards. He addressed his fellow rabbis with the anger of one who had chosen to break ranks: "Do not judge or you too will be judged. For in the same way you judge others, you will be judged, and with the measure you use, it will be measured to you. Why do you look at the speck of sawdust in your brother's eyes and pay no attention to the plank in your own eye? How can you say to your brother, 'Let me take the speck out of your eye,' when all the time there is a plank in your own eye? You hypocrite! First take the plank out of your own eye, and then you will see clearly to remove the speck from your brother's eye."[16]

But then Jesus was not part of a religious establishment; he was a radical. He did not build defensive walls or fear moral contamination. On the contrary, he went to the crossroads and the marketplaces, fraternized with dubious characters, and ate with tax collectors, day laborers, and prostitutes. When the Pharisees wanted him to denounce his sinful brethren, he refused. To my mind, this is one of his most appealing characteristics.

The Greek term used by Jesus in the Gospel is "hypocrite"—yet it is not hypocrisy we are dealing with here, but self-righteousness. The Hebrew word for self-righteousness is *tzadkanut*—the profession of being righteous *(tzedaka)*. At first glance, it looks like a specific kind of hypocrisy—the tendency to present oneself as morally better than one really is.[17] But the hypocrite knows that he is lying. The Greek word *hypokritēs* (used in one form or another in most European languages) referred originally to an actor or mime. The actor knows that he is only playing a role. The tears that he sheds do not come from his heart and the laughter does not come from his belly. He wears a mask. Behind the mask, the *persona,* there is a "real" person. Once the performance is over and the curtain descends, the *hypokritēs* becomes himself again. Of course, some actors remove their mask only rarely, and others are so afraid to take it off that it stays on their face perpetually. But the actor knows, even when he's expressing deep emotion, that it's only theater. "What is Hecuba to him, or he to Hecuba?"[18] When the actor can no longer tell the difference, he passes from hypocrisy to self-righteousness.

The self-righteous are not play-acting. Their personality is not split. They wholeheartedly believe in their make-believe. Their makeup, their mask, has become their skin. They never lose their sense of righteousness (often expressed by chronic indignation), and they never think of themselves except in terms of total sincerity. Even when they know they're lying, they see their lies as part of the complicated and thankless task of serving righteousness. Quick to discern every imperfection in others, the only thing they do not see is themselves. Like the vampire of popular legend, they pass in front of mirrors but their images are not reflected there.

High moral pretensions have gone out of fashion in the West, together with moralizing and fire-and-brimstone preaching. Of course, we still find them on both ends of the political spectrum—among conservatives (old and new) who blame real and imaginary leftists for every evil in the world, and among nature-loving, tobacco-hating, save-the-world liberals. But the vast center has had its fill of moralizing. It has adopted, with great enthusiasm, the ideals of *laissez-faire* and *laissez-passer*. Like Chaucer's Wife of Bath, they do not see their moral mediocrity as a problem. On the contrary, they see it as a God-given right. They do not aspire to be saints, and they fear those who would thrust sainthood upon them. Consumer society wants us to indulge ourselves, so long as we do not harm others—or at least so long as we do not harm business. This is no recipe for holiness. The "mediocre" ethical model is minimalist and pragmatic. Instead of duties, it promotes rights, especially the right to the unimpeded pursuit of happiness. Old solidarities are deconstructed. We are not the Church, or even the Nation (at least not in the way these terms were understood in the past). We are too busy consuming. Save your own soul.

So have we finally gotten rid of self-righteousness? Not quite. It exists wherever individuals and groups feel that they are better than others and apply double standards. In cultures with a strong sense of moral mission, like imperial England in the past (White Man's Burden) or like Israel (Light unto the Nations) and the United States (City upon a Hill; Leader of the Free World) today, people strongly feel that critics are by definition too morally inferior to judge. We are exporting not our goods but democracy and freedom; we are imposing not *our* ethical system but universal values; we love peace, even though we spread it with guns and bombs. If others criticize us, we accuse them of short-sightedness and hypocrisy. We develop morality in reverse. Since we are moral, benign, enlightened nations, the fact that we chose to do something is the best proof of its morality. Deny basic human rights? Invade other countries? Abrogate signed agreements? There must have been good reasons. "How do you sleep after ordering a one-ton bomb to be dropped on the house of a suspected terrorist, killing fourteen innocent people?" the former chief of staff of the Israeli army, General Dan Halutz, was asked by a reporter. "I sleep very well," he answered. "How does it feel?" insisted the reporter. "Well, when the bomb is dropped," the general answered sarcastically, "the pilot feels a slight thump."

We all sleep very well. Every once in a while, we feel a slight thump. And why do we sleep so well? Because we are right and our enemies are wrong; because we are civilized and they barbarians; because our intentions are pure, and our actions must therefore be pure. Of course, accidents happen; but when we choose to investigate them (less often than we would like to think), we feel even better about ourselves. Only upright people like us would remove such insignificant specks from our eyes. Golda Meir, Israel's prime minister in the 1970s and the perfect example of this type of self-righteousness, once declared that she could not pardon the Palestinians for making us do what we did to them. But fear not—her sense of moral superiority remained unshaken.

Finally, a word must be said about the latest form of self-righteousness—the politically correct sort, which is *prima facie* the opposite of the old self-righteousness. If the old type can find nothing wrong with "us," the new type can find nothing right. Politically correct critics direct their arrows against their own culture (the West—more specifically, Western elites), which they often accuse of cultural, economic, and military oppression. It is not the criticism itself that is self-righteous. As the dominant power in the modern age, the West has much to answer for. Self-scrutiny, moreover, is a healthy process (though at times it can turn into ethical hypochondria). What is less commendable is the feeling on the part of the "critical elite" that it is the bearer of special gnosis. Like their many predecessors in history (Manichaean *electi*, Jewish cabbalists, Buddhist masters, avant-garde Bolshevik revolutionaries), they have the ability to see through the thick veil of false consciousness that hides moral reality from the average man and woman. This ability is partly miraculous (certain people have exceptional sensitivities that allow them to see through the Matrix—or through the dominant "discourse," if you prefer) and partly acquired through careful study of the writings of the Enlightened Ones (Michel Foucault, Edward Said, Slavoj Žižek, Judith Butler, to name a few). Having seen the light, they can observe the world with a clear moral eye and denounce anyone who speaks, thinks, or acts otherwise, accusing him (or her) of not being sufficiently sensitive, attentive, ethical.

There is little in all this that is new. It is an attitude rooted in the clerical mindset with which this chapter began (just as Derridean deconstruction is deeply indebted to biblical exegesis). Like more traditional types of self-righteousness, this one involves its own myopia. Rarely do the new critics stop to reflect on the ethical consequences of their critique, on the implicit racism it often reflects ("we cannot expect of others the norms we expect of 'our own kind'"). They almost never recognize the arrogance expressed by their moralizing attitude, not only toward the oppressors, but also toward the oppressed that they claim to ventriloquize, without ever bothering to verify whether the latter are interested in the kind of representation they offer. When you defend the culture of the "other" in the name of "multiculturalism," aren't you often defending the right of the other's elites to continue *their* oppression? When you offer a defense of identity, aren't you often projecting your own anxieties onto others? Are the oppressed interested in the type of egalitarian freedom that you see as ideal?

Even when these questions are raised, they are rarely part of a real dialogue with the other. Elites do not like to mingle too much—hence their use of a complex jargon full of what Erasmus, speaking about scholastics, called "newly coined expressions and strange-sounding words."[19] They rarely admit that their self-righteousness serves primarily their own needs—that it supplies them with moral purpose and ammunition in the power struggle against rival elites, both old and new. In general, their calls to change the world remain confined to university campuses, air-conditioned lecture halls, and the pages of books that no Third World worker, no homeless person, no immigrant will ever read. Nor are they expected to. For the "works" of the new moral critics are an internal affair, destined for prize-nomination committees, for colleagues at other universities, and for the scandal-hungry media. Perhaps the saddest thing about the new critics—who are, like so many self-righteous persons, idealists—is that most of them have lost faith not only in their leaders, but also in themselves. They no longer believe in their ability to change the world and have convinced themselves that words and ideas are more important than deeds. They often denounce, but rarely act. Thus, they combine the vice of pride with the vice of sloth.

I have used the third-person plural throughout this chapter; I wonder if the first-person plural mightn't have been more appropriate. You see, self-righteousness is contagious. To our plank-filled eyes, those specks in yours are quite annoying. You really should do something about them.

11

ADVANCED SIN

I am myself indifferent honest; but yet I could accuse me of such things that it were better my mother had not borne me: I am very proud, revengeful, ambitious, with more offences at my beck than I have thoughts to put them in, imagination to give them shape, or time to act them in.

—SHAKESPEARE, *HAMLET*, 3.1.120

"Our father who is in heaven, I have sinned before Thee. I have trespassed, I have dealt treacherously, I have robbed, I have spoken slander, I have acted perversely, I have done wrong, I have acted presumptuously, I have done violence, I have practiced deceit, I have counseled evil, I have spoken falsehood, I have scoffed, I have revolted, I have blasphemed, I have rebelled, I have committed iniquity, I have transgressed, I have oppressed, I have been stiff-necked, I have acted wickedly, I have dealt corruptly."[1] Very well, I have also been inaccurate: I am not sure I have robbed, done violence, oppressed, revolted, or acted wickedly; I am not sure I know the difference between acting perversely and committing iniquity, between revolting and rebelling, and I am too lazy to check. In addition, I have spoken slander, I have been deceitful,

I have acted presumptuously, I have been stiff-necked, I have betrayed others and myself.

It would have been wonderful to look God and men in the eye and declare loudly: "I am without sin! Here are my entrails and my heart. Examine them at leisure; there is no stain in them." What a marvelous sensation this would have been—to be free of shame, of remorse, of the permanent need to make excuses. On the other hand, I'm not sure I would be able to identify myself with that sinless creature ready to throw the first stone with an untroubled heart and a sure hand. I do not enjoy judging others. In any case, my hands are empty. What would I throw? "One should not appoint anyone to head a community unless he carries a basket of reptiles on his back, so that if he becomes arrogant, one could tell him: 'Turn around.'"[2] I do not wait for people to tell me to turn around. I never forget that my private basket of reptiles is always there, on my back. Our sins make us human.

It is difficult for me to renounce my trespasses. These deadly sins are no longer generic. They are *my* pride, *my* lust, *my* sloth, *my* envy, *my* greed, *my* anger, *my* gluttony, and, yes, *my* self-righteousness. But I also cannot renounce the unforgiving superego that views each and every one of them with holier-than-me disdain. They are not easy masters. But what can I say? "I love my master. . . . I do not want to go free."[3] Or rather, I do not love him, but I do not want to go free either.

The list of our sins is always partial, and any summing up is bound to be incomplete and provisional. So long as a man lives, he yields to temptation. It is impossible to reach the bottom of our bottomless pit of passions and counter-passions. Since, in this book, I have often given accounts of the conscience of others, it is fitting that I conclude with another such account. Here it is, then, in the words of the great Polish poet Czesław Miłosz:

ACCOUNT

The history of my stupidity would fill many volumes.

Some would be devoted to acting against consciousness,
Like the flight of a moth which, had it known,
Would have tended nevertheless toward the candle's flame.
Others would deal with ways to silence anxiety,
The little whisper which, though it is a warning, is ignored.

I would deal separately with satisfaction and pride,
The time when I was among their adherents
Who strut victoriously, unsuspecting.

But all of them would have one subject, desire,
If only my own—but no, not at all; alas,
I was driven because I wanted to be like others.
I was afraid of what was wild and indecent in me.

The history of my stupidity will not be written.
For one thing, it's late. And the truth is laborious.[4]

Am I, like Miłosz, ready to resign myself to my stupidity? Am I ready to declare that it is too late? I'm not sure. Although the basket on my back is full of tailless lizards, I still have my eye on the white whale of happiness.

Notes

All translations are mine unless otherwise indicated.

1. The Lizard's Tail

1. "The fathers eat sour grapes, and the children's teeth are set on edge" (Ezekiel 18:2). All biblical quotations come from the New International Version (NIV) unless otherwise indicated.

2. Richard Bernstein, *Radical Evil: A Philosophical Interrogation* (Cambridge: Polity, 2002), pp. 11–45.

3. Aviad Kleinberg, *Viduim* (Tel Aviv: Yedioth Aharonot, 2001).

4. Augustine, *Confessions,* trans. Henry Chadwick (New York: Oxford University Press, 1991), 2.9, p. 29.

5. Hannah Arendt, *Eichmann in Jerusalem: Report on the Banality of Evil* (New York: Viking, 1963). Naturally, I do not accept Arendt's position.

6. See Kleinberg, *Viduim,* epilogue, pp. 393–431, esp. n. 5. Also Gillian R. Evans, *Augustine on Evil* (Cambridge: Cambridge University Press, 1982).

7. Augustine, *Confessions,* 2.14, p. 32.

2. Sin for Beginners

1. Genesis 1:31. All biblical quotations come from the New International Version (NIV) unless otherwise indicated.

2. Theodor E. Mommsen, "Augustine and the Christian Idea of Progress," in Dorothy Donnelly, ed., *The City of God: A Collection of Critical Essays* (New York: Peter Lang, 1995), pp. 353–372.

3. See *Babylonian Talmud, Shabbat,* 112b: "If the earlier [sages] were sons of angels, we are sons of men; if the earlier were sons of men, we are like asses."

4. Genesis 1:16.

5. Augustine, *The City of God,* trans. Henry Bettenson (New York: Penguin, 2003), 12.4, pp. 475–476. See also Augustine, *The Nature of the Good,* in

The Works of Augustine: A Translation for the Twenty-First Century: The Manichean Debate (New York: New City Press, 2006), 8, p. 327.

6. Matthew 26:23–24.

7. Thomas Aquinas, *Summa Theologiae*, 1a, 2ae, q. 85, art. 3. Jeremy Cohen, "Original Sin as the Evil Inclination: A Polemicist's Appreciation of Human Nature," *Harvard Theological Review*, 73, nos. 3–4 (1980): 495–520.

8. Tatha Wiley, *Original Sin: Origins, Developments, Contemporary Meanings* (New York: Paulist Press, 2002), pp. 56–75.

9. Romans 7:19.

10. Jeremiah 11:20.

11. Romans 9:11–21.

12. Maimonides, "Eight Chapters," in *Ethical Writings of Maimonides*, trans. Raymond Weiss and Charles Butterworth (New York: Dover, 1983), 8, pp. 89–90. On the question of free will, see also Maimonides, *Mishneh Torah*, part 5, "The Laws of Repentance," ch. 5: "That man has free will and [at the same time] God possesses the knowledge of things to come does not undermine the human freedom to choose."

13. This is a phrase from the Kaddish, the Jewish prayer for the dead.

14. Augustine, *The Problem of Free Choice*, trans. Mark Pontifex (Westminster, Md.: Newman Press, 1955), 3.15.44, p. 186.

15. Piero Camporesi, *The Fear of Hell: Images of Damnation and Salvation in Early Modern Europe* (University Park: Pennsylvania State University Press, 1990). Adolf Katzenellenbogen, *Allegories of the Virtues and Vices in Medieval Art* (Toronto: University of Toronto Press, 1989).

16. John 3:16.

17. Augustine, *The Nature of the Good*, 9, p. 327.

18. Jonah 4:1–3.

19. Ibid., 4:10–11. Here I have used the New King James Version, which is closer to the original.

20. Job 4:17–21.

21. Ibid., 14:1–4.

22. Bertrand Russell, "Why I Am Not a Christian," in Jerry H. Gill, ed., *Philosophy and Religion: Some Contemporary Perspectives* (Minneapolis: Burgess, 1968), pp. 133–134.

23. "O felix culpa quae talem et tantum meruit habere redemptorem."

24. Isaiah 14:12.

25. Psalms 22:2 and Mark 15:34.

26. Genesis 4:10.

27. I Corinthians 1:18–29.

28. Genesis 18:25.

29. Romans 9:20–21.

30. "This is what the Lord says to the house of Israel: 'Seek me and live'" (Amos 5:4).

31. Avraham Yitzhak HaCohen Kook, "Yesod Yirat Hao'nesh" (The Foundation of the Fear of Punishment), in *Orot Haqodesh,* vol. 4 (Jerusalem, 1990), p. 417.

32. "Pray for the welfare of the government—for were it not for fear thereof, men would swallow one another alive" (*Babylonian Talmud, Abodah Zarah,* 4a).

33. Oliver Thomson, *A History of Sin* (Edinburgh: Canongate Press, 1993), pp. 42–50.

34. Luke 6:25.

35. Raymond J. Devettere, *Introduction to Virtue Ethics: Insights of the Ancient Greeks* (Washington, D.C.: Georgetown University Press, 2002).

36. Genesis 4:7.

37. Solomon Schimmel, *The Seven Deadly Sins: Jewish, Christian, and Classical Reflections on Human Nature* (New York: Free Press, 1992). Maurice Huftier, "Péché mortel et péché véniel," in Philippe Delhaye, ed., *Théologie du péché,* in *Bibliothèque de Théologie,* ser. 2, vol. 7 (Tournai: Desclée, 1960), pp. 363–451.

38. Evagrius Ponticus, *De octo vitosis cogitationibus,* in *Evagrius of Pontus: The Greek Ascetic Corpus,* trans. and ed. Robert Sinkewicz (New York: Oxford University Press, 2003).

39. Cassian, *Institutiones coenobiorum,* in English *The Institutes,* trans. B. Ramsey, *Ancient Christian Writers,* vol. 58 (New York: Newman Press, 2000).

40. Prudentius, *Psychomachia,* ed. Rosemary Burton (Bryn Mawr, Pa.: College Library, 1989).

41. Morton Bloomfield, *The Seven Deadly Sins: An Introduction to the History of a Religious Concept* (East Lansing, Mich.: State College Press, 1952). Richard Newhauser, ed., *The Seven Deadly Sins: From Communities to Individuals* (Leyden: Brill, 2007).

42. Gregory the Great, *Morals on the Book of Job* (Oxford: J. H. Parker, 1844–1850), 31, 45.

43. Ibid., 34, 23.

44. Lester K. Little, "Pride Goes before Avarice: Social Change and the Vices in Latin Christendom," *American Historical Review,* 76, no. 1 (1971): 16–49.

45. Henry Fairlie, *The Seven Deadly Sins Today* (Washington, D.C.: New Republic Books, 1978).

3. Sloth

1. Siegfried Wenzel, *The Sin of Sloth: Acedia in Medieval Thought and Literature* (Chapel Hill: University of North Carolina Press, 1967). See also idem, "The Seven Deadly Sins: Some Problems of Research," *Speculum,* 43 (1968): 1–27.

2. Robert de Sorbon, "Ad sanctam et rectam confessionem," in *Maxima bibliotheca veterum patrum,* vol. 25 (Lyon, 1677), p. 352.

3. Rabbi Nachman of Breslau, "Menio't" (Obstacles), in *Haetzot Hamevoarot* (Jerusalem, 1995), 7–8, pp. 268–271.

4. *Babylonian Talmud, Berakhot,* 10a. All translations are mine unless otherwise noted.

5. Rabanus Maurus, *De ecclesiastica disciplina,* 3, in *Patrologia latina,* vol. 112, pp. 1251–1253.

6. Cassian, *Institutiones coenobiorum,* in English *The Institutes,* trans. B. Ramsey, *Ancient Christian Writers,* vol. 58 (New York: Newman Press, 2000), 10, pp. 217–234. Petrus Cantor, "Contra pigros," *Verbum abbreviatum,* 79, in *Corpus christianorum, continuatio mediaevalis,* vol. 196, pp. 549–559.

7. Aristotle, *Poetics,* 9.

8. Rabbi Tarfon says: "The day is short; the need is great; the workers are lazy; but the wages are high and the master of the house is impatient" (*Mishna, Avot,* 2.25).

9. See the excellent book by James C. Scott, *Domination and the Arts of Resistance: Hidden Transcripts* (New Haven: Yale University Press, 1990).

10. Genesis 2:15. All biblical quotations come from the New International Version (NIV) unless otherwise indicated.

11. Ecclesiastes 1:12 and 2:4–8.

12. Ibid., 2:11.

13. Ibid., 1:3–9.

14. Ibid., 4:1–3.

15. The expression is drawn from Joseph Karo, *Shulhan Arukh* (The Laid Table), written in Safed in the sixteenth century: "Each man therefore has a duty to make himself strong as a lion. From his waking, he should arise rapidly and be ready to serve our Creator (Blessed Be His Name)" (1:4). Karo's text has become the *vade mecum* of observant Jews.

16. On the roots of modern despair, see Michael Theunissen, *Kierkegaard's Concept of Despair,* trans. Barbara Harshav and Helmut Illbruck (Princeton: Princeton University Press, 2005).

17. Tad Brennan, *The Stoic Life: Emotions, Duties and Fate* (Oxford: Clarendon, 2005).

18. Brad Inwood, "Goal and Target in Stoicism," *Journal of Philosophy,* 83, no. 10 (1986): 547–556.

19. Epictetus, *The Discourses,* trans. C. Gill (London: Everyman, 1995), 1.25.18–22, pp. 56–57.

20. Ecclesiastes holds a contrasting view: "Man has no advantage over animals, for all is vanity" (3:19). On Stoic morality, see Anthony A. Long, *Epictetus: A Stoic and Socratic Guide to Life* (Oxford: Clarendon, 2001); Martha Nussbaum, *The Therapy of Desire* (Princeton: Princeton University Press, 1994); John M. Rist, *Stoic Philosophy* (Cambridge: Cambridge University Press, 1969); and Pierre Hadot, *The Inner Citadel: Meditations of Marcus Aurelius,* trans. Michael Chase (Cambridge, Mass.: Harvard University Press, 1998).

21. "Concerning Benjamin the Righteous, who was a supervisor of the charity fund, it is said that one day a woman came to him in a year of drought and implored: 'Rabbi, feed me.' He replied, 'I swear by God, there is nothing in the charity fund.' She said, 'Rabbi, if you do not feed me, a woman and her seven children will perish.' So he fed her out of his own pocket. Some time afterward, he became gravely ill. The serving angels addressed the Holy One (Blessed Be He), saying: 'Ruler of the Universe, You have said that he who saves a single soul of Israel is to be regarded as if he had saved the entire world.'" (*Babylonian Talmud, Bava Batra,* 11a.)

4. Envy

1. Augustine, *Confessions,* trans. Henry Chadwick (New York: Oxford University Press, 1991), 1.11, p. 9.

2. For general discussions, see Hildegard Baumgart, *Jealousy: Experience and Solutions,* trans. Manfred Jacobson and Evelyn Jacobson (Chicago: Chicago University Press, 1990); David Konstan and N. K. Rutter, eds., *Envy, Spite and Jealousy: The Rivalrous Emotions in Ancient Greece* (Edinburgh: Edinburgh University Press, 2003); Peter Salovey, ed., *The Psychology of Jealousy and Envy* (New York: Guilford Press, 1991).

3. Augustine, *Confessions,* 1.11, p. 9.

4. Proverbs 13:24. All biblical quotations come from the New International Version (NIV) unless otherwise indicated.

5. Augustine, *Confessions,* 1.14.

6. George M. Foster, "The Anatomy of Envy: A Study in Symbolic Behavior," *Current Anthropology,* 13, no. 2 (1972): 165–202.

7. Richard Dawkins, *The Selfish Gene* (Oxford: Oxford University Press, 1976).

8. *Babylonian Talmud, Baba Metsi'a,* 62a.

9. Melanie Klein, "Envy and Gratitude," in Klein, *"Envy and Gratitude" and Other Works, 1946–1963* (London: Hogarth, 1975), pp. 176–233. Herbert Rosenfeld, "On the Psychopathology of Narcissism," in Rosenfeld, *Psychotic States: A Psycho-Analytical Approach* (New York: International Universities Press, 1966).

10. Donald W. Winnicott, *Human Nature* (London: Free Association Books, 1988), pp. 69–78.

11. Ecclesiastes 1:18.

12. Exodus 34:13–14.

13. Ezekiel 16:25–26.

14. Ibid., 23:17–21.

15. Numbers 5:12–15 (New King James Version).

16. Samuel declared that the woman's voice is sexual, since it is said: "For your voice is sweet, and your face is lovely" (Song of Songs 2:14). Rav Sheshet declared that the woman's hair is sexual, since it is said: "Your hair is like a flock of goats" (Song of Songs 4:1).

17. Jacob Neusner, Tamara Sonn, and Jonathan E. Brockopp, *Judaism and Islam in Practice* (London: Routledge, 2000), pp. 67–93.

18. William Shakespeare, *The Tragedy of Othello, The Moor of Venice,* in *The Riverside Shakespeare,* ed. G. Blakemore Evans (Boston: Houghton Mifflin, 1974), 5.2.

19. Livy, *The Early History of Rome,* trans. Aubrey de Selincourt (Harmondsworth: Penguin, 1960), 1.58, 1.99.

20. See Diana C. Moses, "Livy's Lucretia and the Validity of Coerced Consent," in Angeliki E. Laiou, ed., *Consent and Coercion to Sex and Marriage in Ancient and Medieval Societies* (Washington, D.C.: Dumbarton Oaks, 1993), pp. 39–81.

21. Michel Foucault, *The History of Sexuality,* trans. Robert Hurley (New York: Pantheon, 1978).

22. Ya'arah Bar-On, *The Crowded Delivery Room: Gender and Public Opinion in Early Modern Gynecology* [in Hebrew] (Tel Aviv: Haifa University Press, 2000). Susan Broomhall, "'Women's Little Secrets': Defining the Boundaries of Reproductive Knowledge in Sixteenth-Century France," *Social History of Medicine,* 15, no. 1 (2002): 1–15.

23. David M. Buss, *The Evolution of Desire: Strategies of Human Mating* (New York: Basic Books, 1994), pp. 97–122.

24. Miriam Yalan-Stekelis, "Danny the Hero," in Yalan-Stekelis, *"Danny the Hero" and Other Poems* [in Hebrew] (Jerusalem, 1975).

25. Exodus 20:17.

26. *Tamid*, 32a.

27. I Corinthians 7:17, 20–24.

28. Nyanaponika Thera, *Satipatthyma: The Heart of Buddhist Meditation* (Colombo: World Buddhist Publication Committee, 1953).

5. Lust

1. "Tell it not in Gath, proclaim it not in the streets of Ashkelon, lest the daughters of the Philistines be glad, lest the daughters of the uncircumcised rejoice" (2 Samuel 1:20). All biblical quotations come from the New International Version (NIV) unless otherwise indicated.

2. "There she lusted after her lovers, whose genitals were like those of donkeys and whose emission was like that of horses" (Ezekiel 23:20).

3. Judges 5:27, translation modified.

4. Ibid., 5:24–27.

5. Isaac ben Yedaia (Yedaa'iah), *Commentary on Bamidbar Rabba*, 12:8. The text is partly quoted in David Biale, *Eros and the Jews: From Biblical Israel to Contemporary America* (New York: Basic Books, 1992), p. 94; I have modified and completed the translation. For a Christian describing the spiritual dangers of sexual desire, see Galand de Reigny, *Parabolarium*, 16.1.

6. Moses Maimonides, *The Guide of the Perplexed*, trans. Shlomo Pines (Chicago: University of Chicago Press, 1963), 3.49, pp. 601–613.

7. "Most blessed of women be Jaël. . . . He asked for water, and she gave him milk, in a bowl fit for nobles she brought him curdled milk. Her hand reached for the tent peg, her right hand for the workman's hammer. She struck Sisera, she crushed his head, she shattered and pierced his temple. Between her legs he sank, he fell; between her legs he sank, he fell; and where he sank, there he fell—dead." (Judges 5:24–27, translation modified.)

8. "Stolen water is sweet; food eaten in secret is delicious" (Proverbs 9:17).

9. Romans 7:23.

10. *Aboth deRabbi Nathan*, 16.

11. Frances Beer, *Women and Mystical Experience in the Middle Ages* (Woodbridge, U.K.: Boydell Press, 1992). Blair Reynolds, ed., *The Naked Being of God: Making Sense of Love Mysticism* (Lanham, Md.: University Press of America, 2000), pp. 75–96.

12. Bernard of Clairvaux, *Sermons on the Song of Songs*, in *On the Song of Songs I*, trans. K. Walsh, *The Works of Bernard of Clairvaux*, vol. 2 (Kalamazoo, Mich.: Cistercian Publications, 1979), 2.2, pp. 8–9.

13. *Bereshit Rabba,* 55. The Zohar is the most important Jewish mystical text. It is attributed to Rabbi Shimon Bar Yochai, but was written mostly in the late thirteenth century.

14. This story is taken from the thirteenth-century poem by Henri d'Andeli, *Le Lai d'Aristote* (The Lay of Aristotle), ed. Maurice Delbouille (Paris: Les Belles Lettres, 1951).

15. Caroline Walker Bynum, *Metamorphoses and Identity* (New York: Zone Books, 2005), pp. 117–162.

16. Genesis 6:1–4.

17. Deuteronomy 23:2, translation modified.

18. Mary Douglas, *Purity and Danger* (London: Routledge, 2003).

19. Jennifer Wright Knust, *Abandoned to Lust: Sexual Slander and Ancient Christianity* (New York: Columbia University Press, 2006), pp. 51–87. R. Howard Bloch, *The Scandal of the Fabliaux* (Chicago: University of Chicago Press, 1986).

20. Chris Smaje, *Natural Hierarchies: The Historical Sociology of Race and Caste* (Malden, Mass.: Blackwell, 2000), pp. 163–186.

21. Psalms 45:13, translation modified.

22. The Jewish woman has a right to a certain frequency of conjugal relations, variable according to her spouse's profession.

23. Ruth Mazo Karras, "Active/Passive, Acts/Passions: Greek and Roman Sexualities," *American Historical Review,* 105, no. 4 (2000): 1250–1265.

24. Think of the fury that seizes the marquis, Walter, in Chaucer's *Canterbury Tales,* when he realizes that Griselda—his poorest subject, whom he has chosen as wife in the hope that she will never threaten him—is able to play the role of an aristocrat as soon as she changes clothes.

25. Peter Lewis Allen, *The Wages of Sin: Sex and Disease, Past and Present* (Chicago: University of Chicago Press, 2000), pp. 1–24.

26. According to Augustine, the sexual act is impossible without *concupiscentia.* So long as the sex is performed in the conjugal framework, and with the goal of procreation, it is acceptable. There were canonists (notably Huguccio) who believed that the sexual act, even in the conjugal framework, remained a sin. See James A. Brundage, *Law, Sex, and Christian Society in Medieval Europe* (Chicago: University of Chicago Press, 1987), p. 283, n. 11.

27. Kim Power, *Veiled Desire: Augustine on Women* (New York: Continuum, 1996), pp. 216–219. John Bugge, *Virginitas: An Essay in the History of a Medieval Ideal* (The Hague: Martinus Nijhoff, 1975), pp. 5–30.

28. Plato, *Timaeus,* trans. Donald J. Zeyl (Indianapolis: Hackett, 2000), 91b–c.

. Pierre J. Oayer, *The Bridling Desire: Views of Sex in the Later Middle Ages* (Toronto: University of Toronto Press, 1993).

30. Chaucer, "The Wife of Bath's Prologue," *The Canterbury Tales*, trans. Nevill Coghill (Harmondsworth: Penguin, 1951), p. 279.

31. *Babylonian Talmud, Yoma,* 69b.

32. *Babylonian Talmud, Hagigah,* 16a.

33. Jerome, *De perpetua virginitate B. Mariea contra Helvidium,* in *Patrologia latina,* vol. 23, pp. 183–206.

34. I Corinthians 7:1–2, 8–9.

35. John Baldwin, "Consent and Marital Debt: Five Discourses in Northern France around 1200," in Angeliki E. Laiou, ed., *Consent and Coercion to Sex in Ancient and Medieval Societies* (Washington, D.C.: Dumbarton Oaks, 1993), p. 261. See also James A. Brundage, "Implied Consent to Intercourse," ibid., pp. 250–251.

36. *Babylonian Talmud, Kiddushin,* 30b.

37. Song of Songs 5:11–13.

38. Louis Dupré, "The Christian Experience of Mystical Union," *Journal of Religion,* 69, no. 1 (1989): 1–13. Nelson Pike, *Mystic Union: An Essay in the Phenomenology of Mysticism* (Ithaca, N.Y.: Cornell University Press, 1992), pp. 22–40.

39. Plato, *Phaedrus,* trans. H. N. Fowler (Cambridge, Mass.: Harvard University Press, 1972), p. 495.

40. Ibid., pp. 497–499.

41. Plato, *Symposium,* trans. Seth Benardete (Chicago: University of Chicago Press, 2001), pp. 21–22.

42. *Babylonian Talmud, Sotah,* 2a.

43. "For this reason a man will leave his father and mother to be united to his wife, and they will become one flesh" (Genesis 2:24).

44. Lucretius, *De rerum natura,* in English as *On Nature,* trans. W. H. D. Rouse (Cambridge, Mass.: Harvard University Press, 1982), 4.1104–1111, p. 363.

45. *The Letters of Abelard and Heloise,* trans. B. Radice (Harmondsworth: Penguin, 1974), letter 4, p. 133.

6. Gluttony

1. Catherine N'Diaye, *La Gourmandise: Délice d'un péché* (Paris: Autrement, 1996).

2. For Gregory the Great's views on gluttony, see *Moralia in Job,* 30.18, 58–63, *Corpus christianorum, series latina,* vol. 143, pp. 1530–1533.

3. Seneca, "Consolation to Helvia," in *On the Shortness of Life*, trans. C. D. N. Costa (Harmondsworth: Penguin, 1997), pp. 48–49.

4. Candace A. Vogler, *Reasonably Vicious* (Cambridge, Mass.: Harvard University Press, 2002), pp. 74–96.

5. Philippians 3:18–19. All biblical quotations come from the New International Version (NIV) unless otherwise indicated.

6. Caroline Walker Bynum, *Holy Feast and Holy Fast: The Religious Significance of Food to Medieval Women* (Berkeley: University of California Press, 1987). Veronika E. Grimm, *From Feasting to Fasting: The Evolution of a Sin—Attitudes to Food in Late Antiquity* (London: Routledge, 1996).

7. Augustine, *The City of God* (Harmondsworth: Penguin, 2003), 12.17–22, pp. 526–536. Caroline Walker Bynum, *The Resurrection of the Body in Western Christianity, 1090–1336* (New York: Columbia University Press, 1995).

8. Moshe Hayim Luzzato, *Mesilat Yesharim* (Jerusalem, 2001), pp. 244–245.

9. *Babylonian Talmud, Bava Kama*, 79.2.

10. Isaiah 30:19.

11. Cassian, *Institutiones coenobiorum*, in English *The Institutes*, trans. B. Ramsey, *Ancient Christian Writers*, vol. 58 (New York: Newman Press, 2000), 5.18, p. 128.

12. Vincent L. Wimbush, ed., *Ascetic Behavior in Greco-Roman Antiquity* (Minneapolis: Fortress Press, 1990), pp. 66–80.

13. Gillian Clark, *Christianity and Roman Society* (Cambridge: Cambridge University Press, 2004), pp. 60–78.

14. *Kohelet Rabba*, 1.13.1.

15. See Aviad Kleinberg, *Flesh Made Word: Saints' Stories and the Western Imagination*, trans. Jane Marie Todd (Cambridge, Mass.: Harvard University Press, 2008), pp. 81–102.

16. Palladius, *The Lausiac History*, trans. Robert T. Meyer (Mahwah, N.J.: Paulist Press, 1964), p. 33.

17. Thomas of Celano, *Vita prima S. Francisci*, 19.52.

18. Idem, *Vita secunda S. Francisci*, 2.160.211.

19. *Jerusalem Talmud, Kidushin*, 4.12.

20. The English translation in the NIV, "make atonement for him because he sinned by being in the presence of the dead body," is probably correct. But the Hebrew wording can imply that the Nazirite has sinned against his soul.

21. A *nazir* is a man who has vowed to abstain from drinking wine and from cutting his hair. The model *nazir* is Samson.

22. Ecclesiastes 7:16.

23. Maimonides, *Mishneh Torah*, "Hilchot Deot," 3a.

24. *Regula S. Benedicti,* 49.

25. Adalbert de Vogüé, "Travail et alimentation dans les Règles de Saint Benoît et du Maître," *Revue Bénédictine,* 74 (1964): 242–251.

26. Palladius, *The Lausiac History*, p. 63, translation modified.

27. Raymond of Capua, *Vita S. Catharinae*, 2.4.

28. See Teresa M. Shaw, *The Burden of the Flesh: Fasting and Sexuality in Early Christianity* (Minneapolis: Fortress Press, 1998). Also Bynum, *Holy Feast and Holy Fast.*

29. Rudolph Bell, *Holy Anorexia* (Chicago: University of Chicago Press, 1985).

30. Ellen Ross, "'She Wept and Cried Right Loud for Sorrow and for Pain': Suffering, the Spiritual Journey, and Women's Experience in Late Medieval Mysticism," in Ulrike Wiethaus, ed., *Maps of Flesh and Light* (Syracuse, N.Y.: Syracuse University Press, 1993), pp. 45–59.

31. Michelle Mary Lelwica, *Starving for Salvation: The Spiritual Dimensions of Eating Problems among American Girls and Women* (New York: Oxford University Press, 1999); Margaret R. Miles, "Religion and Food: The Case of Eating Disorders," *Journal of the American Academy of Religion*, 63, no. 3 (1995): 549–564.

32. Anthony Synnott, "Tomb, Temple, Machine and Self: The Social Construction of the Body," *British Journal of Society*, 43, no. 1 (1992): 79–110.

33. Information is from websites with OECD and World Health Organization data—for example, choicesmagazine.org/2004-3/obesity/2004-3-02.htm.

34. See Hillel Schwartz, *Never Satisfied: A Cultural History of Fantasies and Fat* (New York: Free Press, 1986).

35. *Tract Gehenom.*

36. *Koran*, trans. N. J. Dawood (Harmondsworth: Penguin, 2003), Surah 37:64–67.

37. See Herman Pleij, *Dreaming of Cockaigne: Medieval Fantasies of the Perfect Life* (New York: Columbia University Press, 2001). Leif Sondergaard, "Far West of Spain: The Land of Cockaigne," in Leif Sondergaard and Rasmus Thoring Hansen, eds., *Monsters, Marvels and Miracles: Imaginary Journeys and Landscapes in the Middle Ages* (Odense: University Press of Southern Denmark, 2005), pp. 173–208.

7. Greed

1. Max Weber, "Religious Rejections of the World and Their Directions," in *Essays in Sociology,* trans. H. H. Gerth and C. Wright Mills (London: K. Paul, Trench, Trubner, 1947), p. 331.

2. Georg Simmel, *The Philosophy of Money* (London: Routledge, 2004), pp. 59-72.

3. See *Babylonian Talmud, Kiddushin,* 71a: "Rabbi Yehoshua ben Levi said: 'Money purifies *mamzerim* [bastards].'"

4. Ecclesiastes 10:20. All biblical quotations come from the New International Version (NIV) unless otherwise indicated.

5. Ibid., 5:9.

6. Joseph Shatzmiller, *Shylock Reconsidered: Jews, Moneylending, and Medieval Society* (Berkeley: University of California Press, 1990).

7. Quoted in Jacques Le Goff, *Your Money or Your Life: Economy and Religion in the Middle Ages,* trans. Patricia Ranum (New York: Zone Books, 1988), p. 60.

8. Matthew 6:24.

9. Ibid., 11:18-19.

10. John 8:7.

11. Ibid., 8:10-11.

12. Luke 6:20, 24.

13. Ibid., 16:25.

14. Matthew 19:17-19 (New King James Version).

15. Ibid., 19:20-21.

16. Ibid., 19:22-24.

17. Luke 6:20. Matthew 5:3.

18. Robert Markus, *The End of Ancient Christianity* (Cambridge: Cambridge University Press, 1990), pp. 157-176.

19. Harold A. Drake, *Constantine and the Bishops: The Politics of Intolerance* (Baltimore: Johns Hopkins University Press, 2000), pp. 72-110. Johannes Roldanus, *The Church in the Age of Constantine: The Theological Challenges* (London: Routledge, 2006), pp. 114-151.

20. *Babylonian Talmud, Avoda Zara,* 4a.

21. William R. Stevenson, *Christian Love and Just War: Moral Paradox and Political Life in Saint Augustine and His Modern Interpretations* (Macon, Ga.: Mercer University Press, 1987), pp. 77-113.

22. *Babylonian Talmud, Taanit,* 16a.

23. Liturgical poetry sung on Saturday evening. See Genesis 22:17: "I will

surely bless you and make your descendants as numerous as the stars in the sky and as the sand on the seashore."

24. The abrogation of debts occurred every seven years and the redistribution of land every fifty years (jubilee).

25. I Timothy 6:7–10.

26. Richard Newhauser, *The Early History of Greed: The Sin of Avarice in Early Medieval Thought and Literature* (Cambridge: Cambridge University Press, 2000), pp. 172–193.

27. Luke 6:20, 24.

28. Lester K. Little, *Religious Poverty and the Profit Economy in Medieval Europe* (London: P. Elek, 1978).

29. Malcolm D. Lambert, *Franciscan Poverty: The Doctrine of the Absolute Poverty of Christ and the Apostles in the Franciscan Order, 1210–1323* (London: Society for Promoting Christian Knowledge, 1961).

30. John Moorman, *A History of the Franciscan Order: From Its Origins to the Year 1517* (Oxford: Clarendon, 1968).

31. The *goy* (gentile, non-Jew) was permitted to work on the Sabbath. He could thus perform for Jews the work that was forbidden them on the day of rest.

32. Michel Mollat, *The Poor in the Middle Ages: An Essay in Social History,* trans. Arthur Goldhammer (New Haven: Yale University Press, 1986).

33. Pope John XXII, "Ad conditorem canonum," "Cum inter nonnullos," and "Quia quorundam mentes," all in *Extravagantes Johannis XXII,* ed. J. Tarrant (Vatican City, 1983), pp. 228–287.

34. Max Weber, *The Protestant Ethic and the Spirit of Capitalism,* trans. Stephen Kalberg (Los Angeles: Roxbury, 2002).

35. Matthew 25:16–29 (New King James version).

36. Adam Smith, *The Wealth of Nations* (New York: Modern Library, 1937), book 4, ch. 2, p. 423.

37. James M. Childs, Jr., *Greed: Economics and Ethics in Conflict* (Minneapolis: Fortress Press, 2000), pp. 1–12.

38. Michael Novak, "Seven Theological Facts," in Novak, ed., *Capitalism and Socialism: A Theological Inquiry* (Washington, D.C.: American Enterprise Institute, 1979), pp. 109–123.

8. Anger

1. Homer, *Iliad,* trans. Robert Fagles (New York: Viking, 1990), 1.1–6.

2. Ibid., 1.69.

3. Ibid., 1.103–104.

4. Ibid., 1.180–187.

5. Ibid., 1.188–200.

6. Aristotle, *Rhetoric*, in *The Complete Works of Aristotle: The Revised Oxford Translation*, ed. Jonathan Barnes, vol. 2 (Princeton: Princeton University Press, 1984), 2.2.1378a31–33, p. 2195.

7. *Iliad*, 1.225–244.

8. Mihnea Moldoveanu and Nitin Nohria, *Master Passions: Emotion Narrative and the Development of Culture* (Cambridge, Mass.: MIT Press, 2002), pp. 123–129.

9. Robert Winston, *Human Instinct* (London: Bantam, 2002), pp. 21–25, 209–245.

10. John J. Medina, *The Genetic Inferno: Inside the Seven Deadly Sins* (Cambridge: Cambridge University Press, 2000), pp. 190–229.

11. William V. Harris, *Restraining Rage: The Ideology of Anger Control in Classical Antiquity* (Cambridge, Mass.: Harvard University Press, 2001).

12. Cassian, *Institutiones coenobiorum*, in English *The Institutes*, trans. B. Ramsey, *Ancient Christian Writers*, vol. 58 (New York: Newman Press, 2000), 8.11, pp. 198–199.

13. Daniel Boyarin, *Unheroic Conduct: The Rise of Heterosexuality and the Invention of the Jewish Man* (Berkeley: University of California Press, 1997).

14. Aristotle, *Nicomachaean Ethics*, trans. Christopher Rowe (Oxford: Oxford University Press, 2002), 7.6.1149a24–1149b3, pp. 197–198.

15. Eugene Vance, *Mervelous Signals: Poetics and Sign Theory in the Middle Ages* (Lincoln: University of Nebraska Press, 1986), pp. 51–85.

16. *The Song of Roland*, trans. Frederick Goldin (New York: Norton, 1978), lays 20–22.

17. Ibid., lay 273.

18. Ibid., lay 131.

19. Ibid., lay 112, line 1465.

20. *Nicomachaean Ethics*, 7.6.1149b13–15.

21. Harvey Milk was the first openly gay city supervisor in San Francisco. In 1978 he was assassinated. His assassin claimed that he had been made mentally unstable by consuming junk food, like Twinkies. He was convicted of voluntary manslaughter and sentenced to seven years and eight months with parole.

22. Numbers 11:1. All biblical quotations come from the New International Version (NIV) unless otherwise indicated.

23. Ibid., 11:10.

24. Ibid., 11:33.
25. Ibid., 12:9.
26. Ibid., 14:15–16. Bryce Edward Baloian, *Anger in the Old Testament* (New York: Peter Lang, 1992).
27. Psalms 79:6–7, 10.
28. Cassian, *Institutiones*, 8.4.1, p. 194.

9. Pride

1. Matthew 19:16–17. All biblical quotations come from the New International Version (NIV) unless otherwise indicated.
2. Virgil, *Aeneis*, in English as *The Aeneid*, trans. Robert Fagles (New York: Viking, 2006), 6.851–853.
3. Psalms 92:1.
4. Augustine, *De civitate dei*, in English as *The City of God*, trans. H. Bettenson (Harmondsworth: Penguin, 1972), 12.6–7, pp. 477–480.
5. Ibid., 9.13, p. 445.
6. Isaiah 14:12. In Hebrew the rebel's name, Heillel ben Shahar, is not one of the names of Satan.
7. Ibid., 14:12–15.
8. Genesis 1:26.
9. *Mishnah, Pirkei Avot*, 3.1, in *The Ethics of the Sages*, ed. Ronald Pies (Northvale, N.J.: Jason Aronson, 2000), p. 127.
10. Deuteronomy 6:4–7.
11. Thomas Aquinas, *Summa Theologiae*, 1a2ae, q. 84.
12. Simone Weil, "Self-Effacement," in Weil, *Gravity and Grace*, trans. Arthur Wills (Lincoln: University of Nebraska Press, 1997).
13. Laozi, *Tao-te-ching*, annotated and explained by Derek Lin (Woodstock, Vt.: Skylight Paths, 2006), 37, 56. Kaliprasada P. Sinha, *The Self in Indian Philosophy* (Calcutta: Punthi Pustak, 1991).
14. Buddhaghosa, *Visuddhimagga: The Path of Purification*, trans. Bhikkhu Nanamoli (Seattle: Pariyatti Editions, 1999), p. 472.
15. Meister Eckhart, sermon 52, "Beati pauperes spiritu."
16. Franz Kafka, *Wedding Preparations in the Country, and Other Posthumous Prose Writings*, trans. Ernst Kaiser and Eithne Wilkins (London: Secker and Warburg, 1954), Third Octavo Notebook, p. 100.
17. Genesis 6:5–6, translation modified.
18. Ibid., 8:21.
19. Ibid., 11:4.
20. Ibid., 8:21, translation modified.

21. Ibid., 9:15.

22. Isaiah 13:9–11.

23. See Aviad Kleinberg, "For No Man Can See Me and Remain Alive" (in Hebrew), in Shlomo Biderman and Rina Lazar, eds., *Nekudat Ha-ivaron* (Tel Aviv: Hakibbutz Hameuchad, 2005), pp. 15–17.

24. "When Rabbi [Yehuda] died, troubles were multiplied twofold. When Rabbi died, humility and fear of sin ceased." Rabbi Yossef said to the teacher: "Do not speak of the death of humility—because I am still around!" (*Babylonian Talmud, Sota*, 49b.)

25. Ibid., *Baba Kama*, 117a.

26. Ibid., *Taanit*, 20a–b.

27. Ibid., *Baba Metzia*, 58b.

10. Self-Righteousness

1. "You are righteous Lord, when I bring a case before you. Yet I would speak with you about your justice: Why does the way of the wicked prosper?" (Jeremiah 12:1). All biblical quotations come from the New International Version (NIV) unless otherwise indicated.

2. Psalms 104:35, translation modified.

3. John 14:6.

4. Ignatius of Loyola, *The Spiritual Exercises*, 366, "Rules for Thinking, Judging, and Feeling with the Church," 14.

5. *Babylonian Talmud, Baba Metzia*, 59b.

6. Matthew 16:18–19, New King James Version.

7. *Patrologia latina*, vol. 217, p. 658.

8. *Babylonian Talmud, Berakhot*, 6b.

9. Deuteronomy 17:11.

10. Moses Nachmanides, *Peroush ha-Torah* (Commentary on the Torah).

11. Hostiensis, *Lectura*, X.2.1.12, s.v. "Per alios," fol. 221v–222r; X.2.22.15, s.v. "Cum tabelio," fol. 347r.

12. *Babylonian Talmud, Sukkah*, 52a.

13. Bernard Gui, *Manuel de l'inquisiteur*, 2 vols., ed. and trans. G. Mollat (Paris, 1926), vol. 1, p. 6.

14. Ibid.

15. Leviticus 19:16, translation modified.

16. Matthew 7:1–5.

17. Bela Szabados and Eldon Soifer, *Hypocrisy: Ethical Investigations* (Peterborough, Ontario: Broadview Press, 2004), pp. 255–270.

18. William Shakespeare, *The Tragedy of Hamlet, Prince of Denmark,* in *The Riverside Shakespeare,* ed. G. Blakemore Evans (Boston: Houghton Mifflin, 1974), 2.2.

19. Erasmus, *Praise of Folly,* trans. B. Radice (Harmondsworth: Penguin, 1985), 53, p. 153.

11. Advanced Sin

1. The list is part of the Yom Kippur prayers.

2. *Babylonian Talmud, Yoma,* 22b.

3. Exodus 21:5. All biblical quotations come from the New International Version (NIV) unless otherwise indicated.

4. Czesław Miłosz, *New and Collected Poems, 1931–2001* (New York: Ecco, 2001), 395

Index

Abelard and Heloise, 80
Adam and Eve: Fall of, 10, 12, 14, 15, 18, 22–23, 28, 29, 36, 44, 45–46, 49, 72, 73, 103, 136–137, 138, 140; and envy, 49; creation of, 133, 136; pride of, 136
Adultery, 50–55, 100–101
Akavya, son of Mahalalel, Rabbi, 137
Akiva, Rabbi, 47, 154
Alexander the Great and Phyllis, 67–68
Amos, Book of, quotation from, 169n31
Angels, 133–135, 136, 137, 140
Anger, 3, 30, 83, 113–131, 151; vs. jealousy, 46; Achilles' wrath, 113–116, 117, 119, 125–126, 127; Aristotle on, 115, 120–121, 124, 126; and culture, 117–120, 126–129; and human reason, 120–121, 125–129; and *La Chanson de Roland*, 121–126, 127–128; vs. envy, 127; vs. gluttony, 127; of God, 129–131, 135, 141; vs. pride, 133
Anorexia, 91–92
Arendt, Hannah, on evil, 167n5
Ariel, Meir (Israeli songwriter), "Song of Pain," 57

Aristotle, 72; *Poetics*, 33–34; on poetry vs. history, 33–34; and Alexander the Great, 67–68; *Rhetoric*, 115; on anger, 115, 120–121, 124, 126; on human reason, 120–121, 126
Arrogance, 143, 146, 147, 161, 164. *See also* Pride
Augustine, Saint: on human nature, 5–6, 8; on evil, 5–7, 8; on stealing pears, 5–8, 14; *Confessions*, 5–8, 45; on God, 6–7, 19, 25; on divine grace, 19; on divine justice, 19; on grace, 25; on original sin, 44, 45–46; on babies, 44–45, 47; on rebellion of angels, 133–134; *City of God*, 134; on Adam and Eve, 136; on sexuality, 174n26
Aurelius, Marcus, 41
Autobiography and sin, 2–9, 33–34, 95–96, 143–146, 147–148, 157

Bar Yochai, Rabbi Shimon, 174n13; on love, 67
Beauty: and ugliness, 11, 19; and lust, 76
Bell, Rudolph, *Holy Anorexia*, 91–92
Benedict, Saint, Rule of, 88, 89–90
Bernard of Clairvaux, Saint, on Song of Songs, 67

185

INDEX

Buddhism, 61; the *atman* in, 138; Nirvana in, 138
Butler, Judith, 161

Cain, 29
Cassian, John, 30, 84, 118
Cassius (Roman consul), 61
Catherine of Siena, Saint, 90–91, 92
Catholic Church: on God's punishment, 26–27; on God's grace and good works, 27; on human moral abilities, 28; on confession of sin, 29; on venial sins vs. mortal sins, 29; and seven deadly sins, 29–31; celibacy in, 75; monasticism in, 88, 89–90; relations with the state, 104; relations with Franciscans, 107–108; John XXII, 108; Innocent III, 153; papal authority/*magisterium*, 153, 155; the Inquisition, 156–157. *See also* Christianity
Change in created world, 10–11
Chanson de Roland, 121–126, 127–128, 130
Charity, 99–100, 171n21
Chaucer's *Canterbury Tales*: Wife of Bath, 74, 159; Walter and Griselda, 174n24
Children: infantile narcissism, 3; envy in, 44–45, 47–48; education of, 45, 46, 49
Christianity: original sin, 10, 12, 14, 15, 18, 22–23, 28, 29, 44, 45–46, 49, 72, 73, 103, 136–137, 138; salvation in, 12–13, 19, 22–24, 25–27, 99–100, 101–102, 105–106, 107, 108; vs. Judaism, 22, 24–26, 27–28, 50, 74–75, 76, 86–87,

104–105, 130, 151–152, 153–154, 155–156; Kingdom of Heaven, 26, 59, 74–75, 83, 100, 102–103, 104, 153; love of God in, 28; virtue in, 28; love of neighbor in, 28, 102; repentance in, 29; baptism, 29, 45–46, 103; vs. Stoicism, 41, 42; vs. Islam, 50, 76, 95, 104, 151–152; asceticism in, 72, 84–93, 100, 105–108; Church Fathers, 73, 83, 87–88; lust in, 74–75; soul and body in, 82–93, 95; Great Persecution, 84–85; Heaven in, 94; and usury, 98–100, 106, 109–110; and poverty, 101–103, 105–110; as Roman state religion, 103–104, 105; and violence, 104. *See also* Catholic Church; Jesus Christ
Cockaigne, Land of, 95
Collatinus, Lucius, 54–55
Communism, 36, 111
Constantine the Great, 85, 103, 105
Consumerism, 58–61, 93, 159
Contentment, 59–61
Culture, 1–2, 29, 55–57; and anger, 117–120, 126–129

Dawkins, Richard, on the selfish gene, 46
Deconstruction, 161
Derrida, Jacques, 161
Despair, as moral sloth, 30
Deuteronomy, 154–155
Discord, 30
Dorotheus, 85
Double standards, 155–158, 159–160

Ecclesiastes: and sloth, 37–39; on vanity, 37–38, 171n20; on self-de-

186

INDEX

Jacob and Esau, 16
Jaël and Sisera, 65, 173n7
Jeremiah, on God's justice, 182n1
Jesus Christ: Last Supper, 12; as
    Savior, 12–13, 19, 22–24, 27; and
    Judas Iscariot, 12–13, 26, 32; as
    Lamb of God, 22–23; Crucifix-
    ion, 23–24, 25, 90, 103, 118, 130;
    on Kingdom of Heaven, 59,
    102–103, 105; as Incarnation, 76,
    137; Resurrection, 83, 85; fast of
    forty days, 91; on greed, 100, 101;
    and adulterous woman, 100–101;
    on Ten Commandments,
    101–102; on the rich, 101–102,
    105, 107; on poverty, 101–102,
    105, 107, 108, 109, 139; Sermon
    on the Mount, 102; on God and
    Caesar, 103–104; parable of the
    talents, 109–110; and anger, 118;
    on turning the other cheek, 118;
    on God's goodness, 132; as
    Truth, 151; on Peter and the
    church, 153; on judgment of
    others, 157–158
Job, Book of, 7; Eliphaz of Teman in,
    20–21; Job in, 21–22
John the Baptist, 100
John XXII, 108
Jonah, Book of, 18–20
Judaism: vs. Christianity, 22, 24–26,
    27–28, 50, 74–75, 76, 86–87,
    104–105, 130, 151–152, 153–154,
    155–156; the Covenant in, 24–25;
    Talmud, 46–47, 79, 142, 145,
    146–147, 155, 167n3, 169n32,
    171n21, 182n24; vs. Islam, 50,
    73–74, 76, 94–95, 104, 151–152;
    jealous husbands in, 50–53;
    circumcision in, 62–66, 68, 74;

the Zohar, 67, 174n13; procre-
    ation in, 73–74; commandments
    in, 74, 101–102, 104–105, 137,
    154–155, 157; *shmita* (abrogation
    of debts) and *yovel* (jubilee law)
    in, 104–105, 179n24; the Sabbath
    in, 108, 179n31; the Diaspora,
    119; prayer of *Shema*, 137; Torah,
    151–153, 154; Halakha, 152–153,
    157; authority of sages in,
    153–155; Yom Kippur, 163–164;
    the Kaddish, 168n12; and Karo's
    Shulhan Arukh, 170n15
Judas Iscariot, 12–13, 26, 32
Judges, Book of, Jaël in, 65, 173n7
Judgment Day, 130, 141–142, 150

Kafka, Franz, *Octavo Notebooks*, 140
Kahana, Rav, 145, 172n16
Kant, Immanuel, 5
Karo, Joseph, *Shulhan Arukh*, 170n15

Leisure, 36–37
Leonardo da Vinci, 142
Lincoln, Abraham, 127
Loricato, Lorenzo, Saint, 85
Love: of neighbor, 28, 102; for God,
    66–67, 75–76, 134; of self, 134,
    135, 137–138
Lucifer/Satan, 82, 83; pride of, 134,
    135, 136
Lucretia (wife of Lucius Collatinus),
    54–55
Lucretius, *De rerum natura*, 79
Luke, Gospel of, Kingdom of Heaven
    in, 102
Lust, 30, 62–80, 87; vs. jealousy, 46;
    Isaac ben Yedaa'ih on, 62–67, 68,
    70, 72, 74, 76; and circumcision,
    62–67, 68, 76; and social